Other titles in the series

Meeting the Needs

of Your Most Able Pupils:

ENGLISH

Erica Glew

Routledge
Taylor & Francis Group

LONDON AND NEW YORK

First published 2007 by
Routledge
2 Park Square, Milton Park, Abingdon, Oxon OX14 4RN

Simultaneously published in the USA and Canada by
Routledge
270 Madison Ave, New York, NY 10016

Routledge is an imprint of Taylor & Francis, an informa business

British Library Cataloguing in Publication data
A catalogue record for this book is available from the British Library

Library of Congress Cataloging in Publication Data
A catalog record has been requested

ISBN 13: 978 1 84312 261 6 (pbk)
ISBN 13: 978 0 203 93232 2 (ebk)
ISBN 10: 1 84312 261 6 (pbk)
ISBN 10: 978 0 203 93232 2 (ebk)

Series production editors: Sarah Fish and Andrew Welsh
Typeset by Servis Filmsetting Ltd, Manchester
Printed and bound in Great Britain
by Bell & Bain Ltd, Glasgow

Contents

Acknowledgements

I am extremely grateful to the following for their support, interest and help while preparing and writing this book.

Sheila Greaves, who contributed extensively to Chapter 4 of this book. Sheila has taught in a range of primary and secondary schools, as well as working as a home tutor and in a special educational unit. She is a member of the secondary consultancy team for Cheshire and has worked in secondary schools supporting colleagues in Key Stage 3 English. Sheila would like to thank the following for their help and support: Coppenhall High School, Crewe; St Gregory's Catholic High School, Warrington; Sandbach High School and Sixth Form College, Cheshire; Sandbach School, Cheshire; Tatton Park – Cheshire County Council; The Bishop's Blue Coat High School, Chester.

Mike Fleetham of www.thinkingclassroom.co.uk for his permission to include his Multiple Intelligences Pupil Questionnaire; Dr Sarah James of the English Faculty at Cambridge University; Professor Deborah Eyre, director of the National Academy for Gifted and Talented Youth; Julie Viens at Project Zero, Harvard University, for her 'leads' on multiple intelligences.

Peter Wickert, headteacher at The Holy Trinity School, Crawley, West Sussex, for creating the opportunities for me to learn so much; and Dr James Kilmartin, assistant headteacher at The Holy Trinity School, Crawley, for all his encouragement over the last few years and the great talks we have had about teaching and learning.

My colleague Richard Tyson for our conversations on providing in school enrichment and challenge for our most able pupils and students; Barry Lorimer and all my colleagues in the English Department at The Holy Trinity School, Crawley, past and present, for all the discussions we have had about the teaching of English over the years that have helped to inform this book.

All the wonderful students and colleagues from whom I have learnt so much and with whom I have had the pleasure to spend time over the years.

Jane Evea (West Sussex School Improvement Service) and Ann Bridgland (now lead professional at CfBT, contracted by the government to lead the Young, Gifted & Talented Programme and for many years the inspiration behind the provision of gifted and talented education in West Sussex and East Sussex) for their boundless enthusiasm and encouragement and for the opportunities they gave me without which this book would never have been written.

Sue Reid, for all the help she has given me through the conversations we have had about this book, the good times we have had and much else; and Louise Haile, for all the great talk and laughter we have had over the years.

My family for patiently waiting for me to finish this book before resuming normal life.

Andrew, my wonderfully gifted and talented husband without whom this book really would not have been produced.

Contributors to the series

The author

Erica Glew teaches English throughout the secondary age range to GCSE, AS and A level. She is the gifted and talented coordinator and head of the learning resources centre at the Holy Trinity Church of England secondary school, a specialist comprehensive school in West Sussex. Erica is also an examiner team leader in English Literature at A level. In 2002 she took part in a study visit to Russia to study gifted and talented education in Samara, a UN World Class Centre of Excellence in G&T education. She has been a member of the NAGTY National English Advisory Group and of the QCA English Key Stage 3 National Curriculum Review Group.

Series editor

Gwen Goodhew's many and varied roles within the field of gifted and talented education have included school G&T coordinator, director of Wirral Able Children Centre, Knowsley Excellence in Cities (EiC) G&T coordinator, member of the DfES G&T Advisory Group, teacher trainer and consultant. She has written and edited numerous reports and articles on the subject and co-authored *Providing for Able Children* with Linda Evans.

Other authors

Art

Kim Earle is a former secondary head of art and design and is currently an able pupils and arts consultant for St Helens. She has been a member of DfES steering groups, is an Artsmark validator, a subject editor for G&TWISE and a practising designer jeweller and enameller.

Design and Technology

During the writing of the book **Louise T. Davies** was a part-time subject adviser for design and technology at the QCA (Qualifications and Curriculum Authority), and part of the KS3 National Strategy team for the D&T programme. She has authored over 40 D&T books and award-winning multimedia resources. She is currently deputy chief executive of the Design and Technology Association.

Geography

Jane Ferretti is a lecturer in education at the University of Sheffield working in initial teacher training. Until 2003 she was head of geography at King Edward VII School, Sheffield, a large 11–18 comprehensive, and was also involved in gifted and talented initiatives at the school and with the local authority. Jane has co-authored a number of A level geography textbooks and a GCSE revision book and is one of the editors of *Wideworld* magazine. She is a member of the Geographical Association and a contributor to their journals *Teaching Geography* and *Geography*.

History

Steven Barnes is a former head of history at a secondary school and Secondary Strategy consultant for the School Improvement Service in Lincolnshire. He has written history exemplifications for Assessment for Learning for the Secondary National Strategy. He is now an assistant head with responsibility for teaching and learning for a school in Lincolnshire.

Mathematics

Lynne McClure is an independent consultant in the field of mathematics education and G&T. She works with teachers and students in schools all over the UK and abroad as well as Warwick, Cambridge, Oxford Brookes and Edinburgh Universities. Lynne edits several maths and education journals.

Jennifer Piggott is a lecturer in mathematics enrichment and communication technology at Cambridge University. She is Director of the NRICH mathematics project and is part of the eastern region coordination team for the NCETM (National Centre for Excellence in the Teaching of Mathematics). Jennifer is an experienced mathematics and ICT teacher.

Music

Jonathan Savage is a senior lecturer in music education at the Institute of Education, Manchester Metropolitan University. Until 2001 he was head of music at Debenham High School, an 11–16 comprehensive school in Suffolk. He is a co-author of a new resource introducing computer game sound design to the Key Stage 3 curriculum (www.sound2game.net) and managing director of UCan.tv (www.ucan.tv), a company specialising in the production of educational software and hardware. When not doing all of this, he is busy parenting four very musically talented children!

Physical Education and Sport

David Morley has taught physical education in a number of secondary schools. He is currently senior lecturer in physical education at Leeds Metropolitan University and the director of the national DfES-funded 'Development in PE' project which is part of the Gifted and Talented strand of the PE, School Sport and Club Links (PESSCL) project. He is also a member of the team responsible for developing resources for national Multi-skill Clubs and is the founder and director of the Carnegie Regional Multi-skill Camp held at Leeds Met Carnegie.

Richard Bailey is professor of pedagogy at Roehampton University, having previously worked at Reading and Leeds Metropolitan University, and at Canterbury Christ Church University where he was director of the Centre for Physical Education Research. He is a well-known author and speaker on physical education, sport and education.

Religious Education

Dilwyn Hunt has worked as a specialist RE adviser in Birmingham and Dudley in the West Midlands, and has a wide range of teaching experience. He is currently a school adviser with responsibility for gifted and talented pupils.

Online content on the Routledge website

The online material accompanying this book may be used by the purchasing individual/organisation only. The files may be amended to suit particular situations, or individual learning needs, and printed out for use by the purchaser. The material can be accessed at www.routledge.com/education/fultonresources.asp

01 Institutional quality standards in gifted and talented education
02 English department gifted and talented pupils policy
03 Departmental checklist and action plan
04 Suggested reading list for able pupils
05 Auditing provision for the most able students in English
06 Acceleration checklist
07 Multiple intelligences (MI) profiling
08 The rhetoric game
09 De Bono's hats
10 Year 7 lesson plan – *Dr Jekyll and Mr Hyde*
11 Year 11 lesson plan – *The Turn of the Screw*
12 Year 9 lesson plans – satire
13 Good practice case study – Bad Alice (discussion cards)
14 Good practice case study – murder mystery
15 How to complete a mind map
16 Building a critical vocabulary
17 Characters – useful vocabulary
18 Using Year 9 aims/objectives to accelerate a Year 8 year group
19 Assessment sheet for reading

www.routledge.com/education

Introduction

Who should use this book?

This book is for all teachers of English working with Key Stage 3 and Key Stage 4 pupils. It will be relevant to teachers working within the full spectrum of schools, from highly selective establishments to comprehensive and secondary modern schools as well as some special schools. Its overall objective is to provide a practical resource that heads of department, gifted and talented coordinators, leading teachers for gifted and talented education and classroom teachers can use to develop a coherent approach to provision for their most able pupils.

Why is it needed?

School populations differ greatly and pupils considered very able in one setting might not stand out in another. Nevertheless, whatever the general level of ability within a school, there has been a tendency to plan and provide for the middle range, to modify for those who are struggling and to leave the most able to 'get on with it'. This has meant that the most able have:

- not been sufficiently challenged and stimulated

- underachieved

- been unaware of what they might be capable of achieving

- been unaware of what they need to do to achieve at the highest level

- not had high enough ambitions and aspirations

- sometimes become disaffected.

How will this book help teachers?

This book and its accompanying website will, through its combination of practical ideas, materials for photocopying or downloading, and case studies:

- help teachers of English to focus on the top 5–10% of the ability range in their particular school and to find ways of providing for these pupils, both within and beyond the classroom

- equip them with strategies and ideas to support exceptionally able pupils, i.e. those in the top 5% nationally.

Terminology

Since there is confusion about the meaning of the words 'gifted' and 'talented', the terms 'more able', 'most able' and 'exceptionally able' will generally be used in this series.

When 'gifted' and 'talented' are used, the definitions provided by the Department for Education and Skills (DfES) in its Excellence in Cities programme will apply. That is:

- **gifted** pupils are the most academically able in a school. This ability might be general or specific to a particular subject area, such as mathematics.

- **talented** pupils are those with high ability or potential in art, music, performing arts or sport.

The two groups together should form 5–10% of any school population.

There are, of course, some pupils who are both gifted and talented. Examples that come to mind are the budding physicist who plays the violin to a high standard in his spare time, or the pupil with high general academic ability who plays for the area football team.

This book is part of a series dealing with providing challenge for the most able secondary age pupils in a range of subjects. It is likely that some of the books in the series might also contain ideas that would be relevant to teachers of English.

CHAPTER 1

Our more able pupils – the national scene

- Making good provision for the most able – what's in it for schools?
- National initiatives since 1997
- *Every Child Matters* and the Children Act 2004
- *Higher Standards, Better Schools for All* – Education White Paper, October 2005
- Self-evaluation and inspection
- Resources for teachers and parents of more able pupils

Today's gifted pupils are tomorrow's social, intellectual, economic and cultural leaders and their development cannot be left to chance.

(Deborah Eyre, director of the National Academy for Gifted and Talented Youth, 2004)

The debate about whether to make special provision for the most able pupils in secondary schools ran its course during the last decade of the twentieth century. Explicit provision to meet their learning needs is now considered neither elitist nor a luxury. From an inclusion angle these pupils must have the same chances as others to develop their potential to the full. We know from international research that focusing on the needs of the most able changes teachers' perceptions of the needs of all their pupils, and there follows a consequential rise in standards. But for teachers who are not convinced by the inclusion or school improvement arguments, there is a much more pragmatic reason for meeting the needs of able pupils. Of course, it is preferable that colleagues share a common willingness to address the needs of the most able, but if they don't, it can at least be pointed out that, quite simply, it is something that all teachers are now required to do, not an optional extra.

All schools should seek to create an atmosphere in which to excel is not only acceptable but desirable.

(*Excellence in Schools* – DfEE 1997)

High achievement is determined by 'the school's commitment to inclusion and the steps it takes to ensure that every pupil does as well as possible'.

(*Handbook for Inspecting Secondary Schools* – Ofsted 2003)

A few years ago, efforts to raise standards in schools concentrated on getting as many pupils as possible over the Level 5 hurdle at the end of Key Stage 3 and over the 5 A*–C grades hurdle at GCSE. Resources were pumped into borderline pupils and the most able were not, on the whole, considered a cause for concern. The situation has changed dramatically in the last nine years with schools being expected to set targets for A*s and As and to show added value by helping pupils entering the school with high SATs scores to achieve Levels 7 and beyond, if supporting data suggests that that is what is achievable. Early recognition of high potential and the setting of curricular targets are at last addressing the lack of progress demonstrated by many able pupils in Year 7 and more attention is being paid to creating a climate in which learning can flourish. But there is a push for even more support for the most able through the promotion of personalised learning.

> The goal is that five years from now: gifted and talented students progress in line with their ability rather than their age; schools inform parents about tailored provision in an annual school profile; curricula include a gifted and talented dimension and at 14–19 there is more stretch and differentiation at the top end, so no matter what your talent it will be engaged; and the effect of poverty on achievement is reduced, because support for high-ability students from poorer backgrounds enables them to thrive.
>
> (Speech at National Academy for Gifted and Talented Youth – David Miliband, Minister for State for School Standards, May 2004)

It is hoped that this book, with the others in this series, will help to accelerate these changes.

Making good provision for the most able – what's in it for schools?

Schools and/or subject departments often approach provision for the most able pupils with some reluctance because they imagine a lot of extra work for very little reward. In fact, the rewards of providing for these pupils are substantial.

● It can be very stimulating to the subject specialist to explore ways of developing approaches with enthusiastic and able students.

> Taking a serious look at what I should expect from the most able and then at how I should teach them has given my teaching a new lease of life. I feel so sorry for youngsters who were taught by me ten years ago. They must have been bored beyond belief. But then, to be quite honest, so was I.
>
> (Science teacher)

- Offering opportunities to tackle work in a more challenging manner often interests pupils whose abilities have gone unnoticed because they have not been motivated by a bland educational diet.

  > Some of the others were invited to an after-school maths club. When I heard what they were doing, it sounded so interesting that I asked the maths teacher if I could go too. She was a bit doubtful at first because I have messed about a lot but she agreed to take me on trial. I'm one of her star pupils now and she reckons I'll easily get an A*. I still find some of the lessons really slow and boring but I don't mess around – well, not too much.
  >
  > (Year 10 boy)

- When pupils are engaged by the work they are doing motivation, attainment and discipline improve.

  > You don't need to be gifted to work out that the work we do is much more interesting and exciting. It's made others want to be like us.
  >
  > (Comment of a student involved in an extension programme for the most able)

- Schools identified as very good by Ofsted generally have good provision for their most able students.

  > If you are willing to deal effectively with the needs of able pupils you will raise the achievement of all pupils.
  >
  > (Mike Tomlinson, former director of Ofsted)

- The same is true of individual departments in secondary schools. All those considered to be very good have spent time developing a sound working approach that meets the needs of their most able pupils.

  > The department creates a positive atmosphere by its organisation, display and the way that students are valued. Learning is generally very good and often excellent throughout the school. The teachers' high expectations permeate the atmosphere and are a significant factor in raising achievement. These expectations are reflected in the curriculum which has depth and students are able and expected to experience difficult problems in all year groups.
  >
  > (Mathematics Department, Hamstead Hall School, Birmingham; Ofsted 2003)

National initiatives since 1997

In 1997, the new government demonstrated its commitment to gifted and talented education by setting up a Gifted and Talented Advisory Group (GTAG). Since then there has been a wide range of government and government-funded initiatives that have, either directly or indirectly, impacted on our most able pupils and their teachers. Details of some can be found below. Others that relate to English will be found later in this book.

Excellence in Cities

In an attempt to deal with the chronic underachievement of able pupils in inner city areas, Excellence in Cities (EiC) was launched in 1999. This was a very ambitious, well-funded programme with many different strands. In the first place it concentrated on secondary age pupils but work was extended into the primary sector in many areas. Provision for gifted and talented students was one of the strands.

Strands in the Excellence in Cities Initiative

EiC schools were expected to:

- develop a whole-school policy for their most able pupils

- appoint a gifted and talented coordinator with sufficient time to fulfil the role

- send the coordinator on a national training programme run by Oxford Brookes University

- identify 5–10% of pupils in each year group as their gifted and talented cohort, the gifted being the academically able and the talented being those with latent or obvious ability in PE, sport, music, art or the performing arts

- provide an appropriate programme of work both within the school day and beyond

- set 'aspirational' targets both for the gifted and talented cohort as a whole and for individual pupils

- work with other schools in a 'cluster' to provide further support for these pupils

- work with other agencies, such as Aimhigher, universities, businesses and private sector schools, to enhance provision and opportunities for these pupils.

Funding changes have meant that schools no longer receive dedicated EiC money through local authorities but the lessons learned from EiC have been influential in developing a national approach to gifted and talented education. **All** schools are now expected to adopt similar strategies to ensure that the needs of their most able students are met.

Excellence Clusters

Although EiC was set up initially in the main urban conurbations, other hot spots of underachievement and poverty were also identified and Excellence Clusters were established. For example, Ellesmere Port, Crewe and Barrow-in-Furness are pockets of deprivation, with major social problems and significant underachievement, in otherwise affluent areas. Excellence Clusters have been established in these three places and measures are being taken to improve provision for the most able pupils. The approach is similar to that used in Excellence in Cities areas.

Aimhigher

Aimhigher is another initiative of the Department for Education and Skills (DfES) working in partnership with the Higher Education Funding Council for England (HEFCE). Its remit is to widen participation in UK higher education, particularly among students from groups that do not have a tradition of going to university, such as some ethnic minorities, the disabled and those from poorer homes. Both higher education institutions and secondary schools have Aimhigher coordinators who work together to identify pupils who would benefit from additional support and to plan a programme of activities. Opportunities are likely to include:

- mentoring, including e-mentoring

- residential summer schools

- visits to different campuses and university departments

- masterclasses

- online information for students and parents

- advice on the wide range of financial and other support available to disadvantaged students.

One national Aimhigher project, Higher Education Gateway, is specifically targeted on gifted and talented students from disadvantaged groups. More information can be found at www.aimhigher.ac.uk.

National Academy for Gifted and Talented Youth (NAGTY)

Government initiatives have not been confined to the most able pupils in deprived areas. In 2002, the National Academy for Gifted and Talented Youth was established at Warwick University. Its brief was to offer support to the most able 5% of the school population and their teachers and parents. It did this in a number of ways:

National Academy for Gifted and Talented Youth		
Student Academy	**Professional Academy**	**Expertise Centre**
• Summer schools including link-ups with CTY in USA. • Outreach courses in a wide range of subjects at universities and other venues across the country. • Online activities – currently maths, classics, ethics, philosophy.	• Continuing professional development for teachers. • A PGCE+ programme for trainee teachers. • Ambassador School Programme to disseminate good practice amongst schools.	• Leading research in gifted and talented education.

NAGTY worked closely with the DfES with the latter setting policy and NAGTY increasingly taking the lead in the practical application of this policy – a policy known as the English Model, which, as explained on NAGTY's website, is 'rooted in day-to-day classroom provision and enhanced by additional, more advanced opportunities offered both within school and outside of it'. NAGTY ceased operation in August 2007 and was replaced by the Young, Gifted and Talented Programme (see below).

The Young, Gifted and Talented Programme (YG&T)

In December 2006, the UK government announced the creation of a new programme in England, the National Programme for Gifted and Talented Education (NPGATE), to be managed by CfBT Education Trust and now known as the Young, Gifted & Talented Programme (YG&T). Among the changes proposed are:

- a much greater emphasis on school and local level provision.

- the setting-up of Excellence Hubs – HEI-led partnerships to provide non-residential summer schools and a diverse range of outreach provision, including summer activities, weekend events and online and blended learning models. There will be free places for the disadvantaged.

- the appointment of gifted and talented leading teachers – one for each secondary school and each cluster of primary schools.

- a national training programme for gifted and talented leading teachers organised by the national primary and secondary strategies.

Further information about YG&T can be found at www.dfes.gov.uk/ygt or www.cfbt.com.

Gifted and talented summer schools

Education authorities are encouraged to work in partnership with schools to run a number of summer schools (dependent on the size of the authority) for the most able pupils in Years 6–11. It is expected that there will be a particular emphasis on transition and that around 50 hours of tuition will be offered. Some schools and authorities run summer schools for up to ten days whilst others cover a shorter period and have follow-up sessions or even residential weekends later in the school year. Obviously the main aim is to challenge and stimulate these pupils but the DfES also hopes that:

- they will encourage teachers and advisers to adopt innovative teaching approaches

- teachers will continue to monitor these pupils over time

- where Year 6 pupils are involved, it will make secondary teachers aware of what they can achieve and raise their expectations of Year 7 pupils.

More can be found out about these summer schools at www.standards.dfes. gov.uk/giftedandtalented. Funding for them has now been incorporated into the school development grant.

Regional partnerships

When Excellence in Cities (EiC) was first introduced, gifted and talented strand coordinators from different EiC partnerships began to meet up with others in their regions to explore ways of working together so that the task would be more manageable and resources could be pooled. One of the most successful examples of cooperation was the Trans-Pennine Group that started up in the northwest. It began to organise training on a regional basis as well as masterclasses and other activities for some gifted and talented pupils. The success of this and other groups led to the setting-up of nine regional partnerships with initial support from NAGTY and finance from DfES. Each partnership had a steering group composed of representatives from local authorities, higher education institutions, regional organisations concerned with gifted and talented children and NAGTY. Each regional partnership organised professional training; sought to support schools and areas in greatest need; tried to ensure that all 11- to 19-year-olds who fell into the top 5% of the ability range were registered with NAGTY; provided opportunities for practitioner research and arranged challenging activities for pupils. Under the YG&T Programme, nine Excellence Hubs have been created to continue and expand the work of the regional partnerships.

Every Child Matters: *Change for Children* and the Children Act 2004

The likelihood of all children reaching their potential has always been hampered by the fragmented nature of agencies concerned with provision for them. Vital information held by an agency about a child's needs has often in the past been kept back from other agencies, including schools. This has had a particularly negative impact on the disadvantaged, for example, looked-after children. In 2004, 57% of looked-after children left school without even one GCSE or GNVQ and only 6% achieved five or more good GCSEs (see national statistics at www.dfes.gov.uk/rsgateway/). This represents a huge waste of national talent as well as many personal tragedies.

The Children Act 2004 sought to overcome these problems by, amongst other things, requiring:

- local authorities to make arrangements to promote cooperation between agencies to ensure the well-being of all children

- all children's services to bear these five outcomes in mind when planning provision. Children should:

  - be healthy

  - stay safe

  - enjoy and achieve

  - make a positive contribution

  - achieve economic well-being.

There are major implications for schools in seeking to achieve these outcomes for their most able pupils, especially where there is deprivation and/or low aspiration:

- local authorities to appoint a director of children's services to coordinate education and social services

- each local authority to take on the role of corporate parent to promote the educational achievement of looked-after children. This should help to ensure that greater consideration is given to their education when changes in foster placements are being considered

- the setting-up of an integrated inspection regime to look at the totality of provision for children.

More information can be found at www.everychildmatters.gov.uk.

Higher Standards, Better Schools for All (Education White Paper, October 2005)

Although the thrust of this Education White Paper is to improve educational opportunities for all, there is no doubt that some proposals will particularly benefit the most able, especially those that are disadvantaged in some way.

- Pupils receiving free school meals will be able to get **free public transport** to any one of three secondary schools closest to their homes between two and six miles away. At present, such children have very little choice in secondary schooling because their parents cannot afford the fares. This measure will allow them access to schools that might be better able to cater for their particular strengths and needs.

- **The National Register of Gifted and Talented Learners** will record the top 5% of the nation's children, as identified by a wide range of measures, so that they can be tracked and supported throughout their school careers. At first, the focus will be on 11- to 19-year-olds but later identification will start at the age of 4. As a first step, in 2006 all secondary schools were asked to identify gifted and talented students in the school census. In reality, some authorities had already begun this monitoring process but making it a national priority will bring other schools and authorities up to speed.

- In line with new school managerial structures, **'leading teachers' of the gifted and talented** will take the place of gifted and talented coordinators. Training (optionally accredited) will be organised through the national strategies. Leading teachers will work closely with School Improvement Partners and local authority coordinators to implement G&T improvement plans, and undertake much of the work previously undertaken by school coordinators.

- **Additional training** in providing for gifted and talented pupils will be available to all schools.

- **A national programme of non-residential summer schools** will be organised to run alongside gifted and talented summer schools already provided by local authorities and individual schools.

- Secondary schools will be encouraged to make greater use of **grouping by ability** in order to meet the needs of the most able and to use **curriculum flexibility** to allow pupils to take Key Stage 3 tests and GCSE courses early and to mix academic and vocational courses.

- **At advanced level, a new extended project** will allow the most able students to demonstrate high scholastic ability.

- **Extended schools** (see later section).

- **More personalised learning** (see later section).

More information on *Higher Standards, Better Schools for All* can be found at www.dfes.gov.uk/publications/schoolswhitepaper.

Extended schools

In many parts of the country, extended schools are already operating, but it is intended that schools will become much more central in providing a wide range of services to children, parents and the community. The government intends to spend £680 million by 2008 to facilitate these developments. Ideally these services should include:

- all-year childcare from 8.00am to 6.00pm

- referral to a wide range of support services, such as speech therapy, mental health and behaviour support

- exciting activities, including study support and extension/enrichment activities that will motivate the most able

- parenting support, which might include classes on healthy eating, helping children with homework, dealing with challenging behaviour etc.

- community use of school facilities, especially ICT.

Again, this is an initiative that will benefit all children, especially those whose carers work. However, there are particular benefits for those children whose school performance suffers because they have nowhere to study at home and for those with talents that parents cannot nurture because of limited means.

More information on Extended Schools can be found at www.teachernet. gov.uk/settingup and www.tda.gov.uk/remodelling/extendedschools.aspx.

Personalised learning

As mentioned earlier in this chapter, a key component of current education reforms is the emphasis on personalised learning – maximising potential by tailoring education to individual needs, strengths and interests. The key features of personalised learning are:

- **Assessment for Learning** – Information from data and the tasks and assessments pupils undertake must be used to feed back suggestions about how work could be improved and what learning they need to do next. But the feedback should be a two-way process with pupils also providing information to teachers about factors impeding their learning and approaches that would enhance it. This feedback should inform future lesson planning. For the most able pupils, effective assessment for learning should mean that they move forward with their learning at an appropriate pace and depth, rather than marking time while others catch up.

- **Effective Teaching and Learning Strategies** – It is still the case that many teachers teach only in the way that was most successful for them as learners. There is ample evidence that our most able pupils do not form an homogeneous group and that, in order to bring out their many and varied gifts and talents, we need to adopt a wide range of teaching strategies, making full use of the opportunities provided by ICT. At the same time pupils need to become aware of the learning strategies that are most successful for them, whilst also exploring a broader range of learning approaches.

- **Curriculum Entitlement and Choice** – There are many examples of highly gifted adults whose abilities were masked at school because the curriculum did not appear to be relevant to them. Schools need to take the opportunities afforded by new flexibility in the curriculum, by the specialised diplomas of study being introduced for 14- to 19-year-olds and by partnership with other schools, colleges and businesses to engage their pupils. There are several schools now where more able pupils cover Key Stage 3 in two years. The year that is freed up by this approach can be used in a variety of ways, such as starting GCSE courses early, following an enrichment programme or taking up additional science and language courses. The possibilities are endless if there is desire for change.

- **School Organisation** – Effective personalisation demands a more flexible approach to school organisation. This flexibility might show itself in the way teaching and support staff are deployed, by the way pupils are grouped, by the structure of the school day and by the way in which ICT is used to enable learning to take place beyond the classroom. At least one school is abandoning grouping by age in favour of grouping by ability in the hope that this will provide the necessary challenge for the most able. It remains to be seen how successful this approach is but experimentation and risk-taking is essential if we are to make schooling relevant and exciting for our most able pupils.

- **Partnerships Beyond Schools** – Schools cannot provide adequately for their most able pupils without making full use of the opportunities and expertise offered by other groups within the community, including parents together with family support groups, social and health services, sports clubs and other recreational and business organisations.

The websites www.standards.dfes.gov.uk/personalisedlearning and www.teacher net.gov.uk/publications/ will provide more information on personalised learning, whilst new curriculum opportunities to be offered to 14- to 19-year-olds are described in www.dfes.gov.uk/14-19.

Self-evaluation and inspection

The most able must have as many opportunities for development as other pupils. Poor, unchallenging teaching or an ideology that confuses equality of opportunity with levelling down should not hinder their progress. They should have a fair share of a school's resources both in terms of learning materials and in human resources. The environment for learning should be one in which it is safe to be clever and to excel. These are points that schools should consider when preparing their self-evaluation and school development plans.

There have been dramatic changes in the relationships between schools and local authorities and in the schools' inspection regime since the Children Act 2004. Local authorities are now regarded as commissioners for services for children. One of their tasks is to facilitate the appointment of SIPs, School Improvement Partners, who act as the main conduit between schools and LAs and take part in an 'annual conversation' with their schools when the school's self-evaluation and progress towards targets is discussed.

Self-evaluation is also the cornerstone of the new shorter, more frequent Ofsted inspections, using a SEF (self-evaluation form) as a central point of reference together with the five outcomes for children of *Every Child Matters*. An invaluable tool for schools recognising that they need to do more for their gifted and talented pupils, or simply wanting to assess their current provision, is the institutional quality standards for gifted and talented education (IQS).

Institutional quality standards for gifted and talented education (IQS)

These standards, developed by a partnership of the DfES, NAGTY and other interested groups, are an essential self-evaluation tool for any school focusing on its gifted and talented provision. Under each of five headings, schools look carefully at the level indicators and decide which of the three levels they have achieved:

- **Entry level** – a school making its first steps towards developing a whole-school policy might find that much of its provision falls into this category. Ofsted would rate such provision satisfactory.

- **Developing level** – where there is some effective practice but there is room for development and improvement. This aligns with a good from Ofsted.

- **Exemplary level** – where good practice is exceptional and sustained. Ofsted would rate this excellent.

The five headings show clear links to the personalisation agenda: effective teaching and learning strategies; enabling curriculum entitlement and choice; assessment for learning; school organisation; and strong partnerships beyond school.

Having identified the levels at which they are performing, schools are then able to draw up development plans. A copy of these standards is included in the appendices and more information about them can be found at www2.teachernet. gov.uk/qualitystandards.

Resources for teachers and parents of more able pupils

There is currently an abundance of resources and support agencies for teachers, parents and gifted and talented young people themselves. A few of general interest are included below. Other English examples will be found in later chapters of this book.

World Class Tests

These have been introduced by QCA to allow schools to judge the performance of their most able pupils against national and international standards. Currently tests are available for 9- and 13-year-olds in mathematics and problem solving. Some schools have found that the problem solving tests are effective at identifying able underachievers in maths and science. The website contains sample questions so that teachers, parents and pupils themselves can assess the tests' suitability for particular pupils or groups of pupils, and the tests themselves are also available online. For more information go to www.worldclassarena.org.uk.

National Curriculum Online

This website, administered by QCA, provides general guidance on all aspects of the National Curriculum but also has a substantial section on general and subject-specific issues relating to gifted and talented education, including identification strategies, case studies, management and units of work. Details of the National Curriculum Online can be found at www.nc.uk.net/gt.

G&TWise

G&TWise links to recommended resources for gifted and talented pupils, checked by professionally qualified subject editors, in all subjects and at all key stages and provides up-to-date information for teachers on gifted and talented education. Details can be found at www2.teachernet.gov.uk.

NACE – the National Association for Able Children in Education

NACE is an independent organisation that offers support for teachers and other professionals trying to develop provision for gifted and talented pupils. It gives advice and guidance to teachers and others, runs courses and conferences, provides consultants and keynote speakers.

It has also produced the NACE Challenge Award Framework, which it recommends could be used alongside IQS, as it exemplifies evidence and action planning. While IQS indicates what needs to be improved, the Challenge Award Framework suggests how to effect change. More information can be found at www.nace.co.uk.

National Association for Gifted Children (NAGC)

NAGC is a charity providing support for gifted and talented children and young people and their parents and teachers. It has a regional structure and in some parts of the country there are branch activities for children and parents. NAGC provides: counselling for both young people and their parents; INSET and courses for teachers; publications; activities for 3- to 10-year-olds; and a dedicated area on their website for 11- to 19-year-olds (to which they have exclusive access), called Youth Agency. For further information go to www.nagcbritain.org.uk.

Children of High Intelligence (CHI)

CHI acts on behalf of children whose intelligence puts them above the 98th percentile. It often acts in a support capacity when parents are negotiating appropriate provision with schools and local authorities. For further details visit www.chi-charity.org.uk.

Summary

- Schools must provide suitable challenge and support for their most able pupils.
- Appropriate provision can enhance motivation and improve behaviour.
- Recent legislation to support disadvantaged children should mean that fewer potentially gifted and talented children fall through the net.
- Effective self-evaluation of school provision for gifted and talented pupils and challenging targets are the keys to progress.
- There are many agencies that can help teachers with this work.

Departmental policy and approach

- The role of the subject leader
- Departmental policy for more able students
- Auditing current provision for more able students
- Organisational strategies
- Allocation of resources for more able students
- Liaison with other departments
- Homework policy
- INSET activities

The role of the subject leader

In many schools the management structure of English is being re-organised so that each Key Stage is being led by a Key Stage leader/manager. There might also be leaders for subjects like Media Studies within the English team.

In some schools, someone may be given responsibility for more able pupils in the subject area to give provision a sharper focus and to link with the school's G&T coordinator, representing the department on working/research groups and/or at relevant meetings on G&T issues. The following draft job description may be useful in defining such a role.

Draft job description for departmental gifted and talented/able pupil coordinator

Communication

- Act as the department's link representative on all matters related to the school's provision for its most able pupils.

- Liaise with the school's gifted and talented (able pupil) coordinator and pastoral staff, e.g. tutors and heads of year/house on all issues related to the most able pupils in English.

- Liaise closely with the head of the department and KS leaders on any G&T issues arising.

- Liaise with learning resources centre/library to ensure good stock of challenging reading – fiction, non-fiction and specialist magazines suitable for all age groups (see recommended list on website).

- Liaise with SEN department about any pupils who are very able in any aspect of English but who have special educational needs, e.g. pupils who have ADHD, Asperger syndrome or dyslexia.

- Act as 'point of contact' for parents of the department's most able pupils.

- Liaise with relevant outside support agencies, e.g. local authority advisers, NAGC and NACE.

Identification

- Ensure English staff identify the most able pupils in the subject using the agreed criteria in their observation and judgements.

- Investigate the work of pupils who score highly on the verbal CAT tests but who have not been identified by teachers as being amongst the most able.

- Ensure the school's G&T coordinator is given the names of the subject's most able pupils (including any in the top 5% nationally) for the school's G&T register.

Provision within the English classroom

- Ensure that all units of work in the Programmes of Study at KS3 and KS4 indicate where opportunities for higher order thinking skills are being given.

- Ensure that all teachers of English are provided with details of the most able pupils early in the academic year.

- Ensure teachers are aware of the kind of classroom climate which most effectively inspires and motivates the most able in English.

- Ensure teachers are aware of the repertoire of teaching strategies effective for the most able pupils in English through department INSET and in department discussions.

Outside the classroom

- Ensure there is appropriate enrichment opportunity for the most able pupils in English at both Key Stages 3 and 4.

Monitoring and evaluation

- Ensure that the most able pupils are making good progress and investigate any pupils who are not.

- Conduct evaluation exercises, e.g. questionnaires for pupils and for parents on effectiveness of provision.

Departmental policy for more able students

The English department's policy for its most able pupils needs to be developed within the context of the whole-school policy (Appendix 2.1). It should describe how things work in practice in the department. A guide to what needs to be included can be seen in the example of a departmental policy document in Appendix 2.2 and on the accompanying website.

Auditing current provision for more able students

When considering the effectiveness of the department's policy for its most able pupils, it is important to carry out an audit of current provision so that any gaps in that provision can be identified and addressed. A list of priorities for action to ensure the department is providing effectively for the most able then needs to be drawn up. The departmental checklist and action plan should help to prioritise action (Appendix 2.3). The accompanying website contains a more detailed and comprehensive audit tool.

Recent DfES guidelines suggest that departments need to keep changes to about 15% on the MIC (Maintain, Interim, Change) annually. This is to keep the work involved manageable and effective. It is likely, of course, that G&T priorities for development will be one amongst others that will be identified in the 15% for any given year. Any planned changes then need to be embedded in the annual departmental development plan. It is crucial that priorities for the next year are set so that the direction of development is clear for everyone in the department and enables the school's leadership team to consider any financial implications raised by the plan. It needs to be regarded as a set of aspirations the school and the department will work towards achieving. Changes in circumstances in the year ahead might mean the plan needs to be altered. Any changes in the curriculum by central government or by examinations boards will, of course, also point to modifications.

Organisational strategies

When considering provision for the most able, an English department needs to address a number of organisational issues:

- How should we group students?

- How can we use/introduce more flexible learning pathways for groups of able pupils and individuals?

- How can we make best use of our resources for the most able?

- How should we assess and monitor pupils?

- How can homework be used to enhance their learning?

- What training do we need to enable us to provide effectively for our most able pupils?

Groupings

Setting

The way pupils are grouped within the school, year group and the classroom can have a major impact on whether or not the needs of the most able are met. However, it is important to stress that there is no one right way of grouping pupils. The strategies adopted will depend on many factors including the overall philosophy of the school, its size, facilities, the area it serves and the strengths of its teaching team. In areas where schools have received Excellence in Cities money, there is an expectation that setting will be in place for the core subjects, unless current levels of achievement are high.

English departments might well decide that they do not want to introduce setting as soon as pupils enter the school in Year 7, preferring to monitor and assess their abilities in the various different aspects of English for a while before making any decisions about which sets pupils should be placed in. Some schools might decide to teach Year 7 in mixed ability groups and then set at the beginning of Year 8.

Setting may be broad or fine. There may be parallel top sets or a smaller elite group. The obvious advantage of any form of setting is that lesson planning seems easier as there is a narrower band of ability and the most able may find the general pace of lessons more in keeping with their needs. But there are disadvantages too:

1. There is often a reluctance to move pupils out of top sets to accommodate late developers. When pupils are organised in ability sets these must always be flexible and seen as a means of supporting the needs of **all** pupils. An able pupil who has been wrongly placed initially must be given the opportunity to move between sets. The fact that an error has been made must be acknowledged. The pupil's views on moving sets should be carefully sought in discussion and the reasons for a move explained. If they are happy to move, they should be moved at whatever stage in the year the error is recognised. **Movement between sets must not be left to a single annual event only**. An able pupil in the wrong ability set will suffer boredom and frustration at the lack of challenge. This can lead either to disruptive behaviour, lack of engagement or an intellectual and emotional withdrawal which can, in some cases, result in depression. Similarly, a pupil struggling in a high ability set should be moved to a set more likely to support their particular learning needs. Again, the pupil's own view should be sought in discussion. Often, while one pupil may feel relieved at the opportunity to move, another's self-esteem might be damaged. Clearly, sensitive judgements need to be made based on sensitive discussion with the pupil and the pupil's parents.

2. Those in lower sets can find setting very demoralising and behaviour may deteriorate.

3. Teachers do not always recognise that differentiation is still very important for the top sets. Sometimes the greatest ability range is within these groups, especially in very deprived areas where there might be one or two outstanding students in a top class and many others who will do well to get GCSE grade C.

Mixed ability teaching

Many teachers of English believe, and have demonstrated, that mixed ability teaching can be very successful in this subject and that this approach avoids the 'self-fulfilling prophecy' effect of labelling pupils in particular ways early in their secondary school careers. However, careful planning is essential so that the most able do not mark time while others catch up and tasks are differentiated to provide an appropriate level of challenge. The needs of the most able pupils might be well met in a mixed ability grouping when:

● teachers are committed to this way of working

● there is a rich variety of resources

● teaching assistants are on hand to help in meeting individual needs.

Flexible grouping

The employment of additional support staff is allowing more English departments to adopt a flexible grouping approach. There are many variations but generally pupils in each year have a mixed ability base group but can be re-grouped for specific purposes. This allows teachers to bring the most able pupils in English together to study a particularly challenging text or to work on the skills that will help them to achieve the highest standards at Key Stage 3 or GCSE. It would, of course, give them similar opportunities to work with other groups, including those with SEN or the (often forgotten) 'average' students. The advantage of this approach is that able pupils, who might find themselves in lower English sets because of dyslexia or other difficulties, could be placed with the most able for some activities, especially for listening and speaking tasks or drama where they often excel.

The main disadvantage of flexible grouping is that students and teachers often dislike moving out of the comfort zone of their base groups. A very supportive environment will have to be established to overcome this problem.

Fast tracking and the flexible curriculum

Fast tracking means allowing pupils to move at a faster pace through the curriculum even though they usually remain with their peer group. The most common example is when pupils sit GCSE English at the end of Year 10. However, the department is then faced with the issue of how pupils' progress is sustained in Year 11. This can be tricky and heads of department need to consider:

● if pupils are not assured a very good grade in GCSE English or English Literature when taking either or both of these examinations early, is anything to be gained by this approach? Having said this, some schools have used early entry as a wake-up call for 'coasting' able pupils. If they do well in the examination, that's fine, but if they do not, they have a clearer idea of how much effort they need to put in to achieve a higher grade in Year 11.

- if the department has the resources to support pupils in Year 11 with additional courses, enrichment programmes or the opportunity to start AS level if they intend to study English in the sixth form.

- if the intention is to allow pupils to use the time when they would have been studying English in Year 11 to work, unsupervised, on other subjects, do they have the self-discipline and motivation to do this? Many schools have found that the time is wasted unless pupils are carefully supervised and supported in an identified programme of work. On the other hand, some pupils welcome 'space' in the timetable and relief from the pressure they can often feel as conscientious students who always try to achieve their best. It also gives them more independence to plan their own work programmes. There is no easy answer. These are issues that departments will have to discuss when planning any fast tracking.

- if pupils are planning to take A level English in the sixth form, is it wise to offer no English in Year 11? Might the lack of continuity be disruptive?

Fast tracking can be difficult but where the resources are available there are many courses in English and related subjects that can be offered to Year 11 pupils to maintain momentum and motivation. These include:

- Media Studies and Film Studies at GCSE and at AS and A level

- Drama GCSE and Theatre Studies at AS and A level

- English Language at AS and A level

and/or

- English Language and Literature at AS and A level.

The advent of the 14–19 Strategy and the Key Stage 3 Strategy has seen some interesting innovations. One of the desired outcomes of these initiatives is the reduction of 'prescription' so that schools have:

- the space to stretch their most able pupils

- the freedom to experiment with different subjects and approaches to teaching and learning

- the opportunity to develop subject-related enrichment activities

- the chance to develop courses in partnership with other agencies such as private schools, schools with specialist status, sixth form colleges, art/music schools, and FE colleges.

Excellence in Cities areas have pioneered a number of such teaching initiatives in English and related subjects and it is worth looking at some of these on the DfES Standards and other websites. The Open University Young Applicants in School Scheme (YASS) now offers courses especially designed for able pupils and schools might consider these. More information can be found on the website www.open.ac.uk/yass.

Some schools have been experimenting with a different form of fast tracking by offering a two-year Key Stage 3 programme for classes of able students. This gives them an extra year for their GCSE programme which, in turn, gives them space to fit in additional or more advanced courses.

Case study

The Admiral Lord Nelson School, Portsmouth, is operating acceleration programmes in all subjects. Twenty-five per cent of the school's 1,000 pupils participate in acceleration. The acceleration programmes were introduced two years ago. Individual pupils are assessed on their National Curriculum level, and those achieving Level 5 or better begin their GCSE studies in Year 9, thus reducing Key Stage 3 to a two-year duration. SATs are taken at the end of Year 8 following parental consent.

GCSEs are then taken in Year 10, freeing Year 11 for more independent learning, more distance learning, more vocational qualifications and more courses linked to college. This programme is embraced enthusiastically by all departments, especially Science and English. The acceleration programmes are fully supported by staff at the school.

(DfES 2002, *Gifted and Talented Provision: An Overview*, p. 16)

Further suggestions for how schools and departments can provide a more flexible curriculum for their most able pupils can be found in *Key Stage 3 National Strategy – A Condensed Key Stage 3: Designing a Flexible Curriculum* (DfES and QCA, 2004).

Timetabling a flexible curriculum can be a nightmare and there are school/department budget implications for all innovative teaching and learning which would have to be considered. School/department staffing costs might act as a constraint but good short-term and medium-term developmental planning will enable English departments to set priorities which will gradually be incorporated in the short- and medium-term priorities the department sets for itself.

The greater the degree of flexibility in the English department's curriculum, the easier it is to provide for the interests and abilities of particular pupils in a more personalised way.

Acceleration

Acceleration is a form of fast tracking in that it allows pupils to work through the curriculum at a faster rate. The main difference is that it usually means that the pupil or pupils miss out a school year or more in order to work with older pupils. More often than not, when acceleration is used, pupils move into an older age group for all lessons but there are also occasions when the arrangements apply to only one or two subjects (partial acceleration) and pupils spend the rest of their time with their peers. English departments rarely use partial acceleration, possibly because life experiences and maturity contribute more to exceptional performance in this subject than they do in subjects like mathematics, science or modern foreign languages where the rapid acquisition of specific skills is more often used to justify acceleration.

For some pupils, who are both exceptionally able and also socially, emotionally and physically mature, acceleration can work.

> I had no regrets about being accelerated; I found the work interesting, and I might have been bored if I'd been further down.
>
> (Gifted mathematician aged 19 – Freeman, 2001, p. 192)

But even where it appears to work, there is often a cost:

> I had absolutely no confidence at all and I didn't have any friends. I don't think it was my fault, or that I was spoilt, but the others would spend their time teasing me because they said it was fun – nine-year-old little girls are so cruel. It (acceleration) didn't make it easy for me to grow up, though I think I did gain something while I was going through it . . . My mum tells me I used to come home sometimes from school, crying my eyes out, being so unhappy.
>
> (Same gifted mathematician aged 19 – Freeman, 2001, p. 192)

If, as a member of the English department, a teacher is asked his/her opinion about accelerating a child, it might be useful to refer to the checklist on page 25.

Allocation of resources for more able students

English departments are expected to identify some 5–10% of the school population as gifted or talented in this subject and yet it is often the case that these pupils do not receive a similar percentage of the resources allocated to meeting their needs. A fair share of the departmental budget should be allocated to the most able and a section in the department's policy devoted to how funds are allocated for supporting the needs of different groups within English, e.g. SEN and G&T pupils. It is important that sufficient resources of the right kind are provided for the most able. There can be a tendency to purchase books/texts for the middle of the ability range in the hope of satisfying everyone.

The most able students should also be given a reasonable share of the human resources available to the department and provided with appropriate study support programmes. English teachers need to ask themselves:

- where learning assistants and learning mentors are employed, are they directed to work only with difficult pupils and those with SEN or do the most able also get their fair share of support?

Acceleration checklist

Before accelerating a child, have you:	Yes/No
1. explored all available strategies for providing for that child within his/her peer group?	
2. consulted fully with: • parents (such consultation should include advice on pros and cons of acceleration and time for parents to consider this information) • teachers • the child (children are rarely consulted or involved in the process) • any receiving schools or colleges (are they prepared to accept young pupils? Can they provide appropriate programmes of study for them?)	
3. considered: • the emotional/social maturity of the child? • the physical maturity of the child? • areas of weakness within curriculum (e.g. presentation skills or spelling)? • the friendship ties of the child? • the long-term impact on the child? (e.g. there can be conflict at adolescence between parents and children when children want to socialise with and behave like their classmates and not their chronological age group . . . Is the child likely to benefit from going to university early?)	
4. drawn up a short-term plan with all concerned parties for the pupil's educational provision?	
5. made arrangements for regular review of the pupil's progress throughout his/her schooling?	
6. told parents, child and teachers of agencies (e.g. NAGC Youth Agency) that can support them if there are difficulties?	

- do learning assistants occasionally support other pupils, freeing up the subject specialist to work with the most able?

- is study support at Key Stages 3 and 4 devoted to those borderlining Levels 4/5 and GCSE grades C/D, or are those capable of achieving Levels 8 and outstanding performance or GCSE A* also given appropriate support?

Liaison with other departments

Close liaison with the special educational needs department is crucial to ensure that pupils diagnosed as having, for example, ADHD, Asperger syndrome or dyslexia are properly supported. Where setting arrangements are in place, it is also very important that these pupils' high intellectual ability is recognised and that they are placed in appropriate sets. Suitable equipment such as PCs or laptops and Dictaphones must be made permanently available for these pupils to use in English lessons. Many of our leading universities offer exceptional support to students with ADHD, dyslexia or mental health issues. Schools really do need to ensure that intellectually able students with these difficulties are just as well supported so that they can actually succeed in getting to the universities.

They may well be amongst the most able verbally, for instance, but can often be placed in a low set because of difficulties with concentration. A pupil with ADHD will probably need a learning assistant in English to help him/her focus on writing activities and to intervene on the occasions when his/her behaviour might be troublesome to the flow of the lesson or to other pupils when they are engaged in work.

Collaboration with the ICT department in setting up ICT-based English units at Key Stage 3 can result in an important and fruitful partnership.

Liaison with the learning resources centre/library is also crucial if the needs of our most able pupils are to be met. An introductory unit of work which involves all Year 7 pupils in getting to know the library, learning how to find books, subject-specific magazines and other resources, and developing research skills is important. There needs to be a two-way exchange of information between the English department and the learning resources centre. The staff at the centre need to know who the most able students in English are so that they can be directed towards more challenging resources. They also need suggestions from the English department about what should be purchased for the centre. If the English department is planning a new programme of work or an innovative project of some sort, resource centre staff should be involved in this planning so that they can make provision for the full ability range when pupils arrive in the centre seeking help and advice.

Liaising with other departments such as art, music, history, RS and geography in the development and timing of curriculum topics should also be carried out to extend the scope of the challenge for able pupils, helping them to make connections and pursue lines of interest. The topics do not have to be scheduled at exactly the same time but the timing can be considered in the light of what other departments are teaching and when. Within a term or so of the English department's unit on non-fiction and *The Diary of Anne Frank*, history might be examining the Holocaust in Year 9. When the art department looks at self-portraits and pupils are drawing and painting their own portraits, autobiographical writing in English can be scheduled as a writing unit. At GCSE in English, Martin Luther King's 'I have a dream' speech lends itself to teaching the language of persuasion as does Kennedy's 'Ask not what your country can do for you. . .', and liaison with the history and RS departments in exploring King and the Civil Rights Movement can work alongside the study of *To Kill a Mockingbird*. Liaising with the music and art departments at AS and A2 level on Romanticism, modernism and other periods and movements in the arts – and sharing staff expertise – should also be considered.

Individual learning plans

Sometimes in order to support **exceptionally able** pupils in English, the teacher may liaise with colleagues to draw up an individual learning plan. This needs to be easily accessible to staff on the shared area of the school's intranet so that teaching and pastoral staff are aware of what the programme involves and what arrangements need to be made. The pupil's parents should be provided with a paper copy of what has been agreed. This does not have to be elaborate. It can simply be a schedule of the learning opportunities planned and may be drawn up in response to a meeting with the pupil and his or her parents at which the needs and interests of the pupil are discussed. Access to information about opportunities such as the BBC's writing opportunities; courses offered by YG&T; competitions; The Poetry Society; opportunities in school such as writing circles; or access to special events such as a writer in school, should be outlined in the plan.

Exceptionally able pupils should be given website addresses (Cambridge University's English website http://aspirations.english.cam.ac.uk/converse/home.acds is excellent) and sophisticated reading lists.

Learning diaries

The most able pupils might be asked to keep a learning diary in which they record things learnt – perhaps set by the English G&T link teacher with whom they meet regularly to discuss their learning. This could involve reading or writing challenges or researching. The challenges should start with the pupils' own interests but be designed to take them along unexplored pathways.

> An exceptionally able pupil, who loves to write but who is also interested in classical civilisation, might be asked to research the life of women in Ancient Greece and an important historical figure such as Socrates. The pupil may then write a story or a beginning chapter for a novel set in Ancient Greece involving these elements. A pupil interested in modern history might research Cold War politics and create a story, the beginning for a film script or a chapter for a book in the spy genre. A pupil also talented in, say, basketball or art or music could be challenged to write a television script for an episode within some aspect of these worlds.

These pupils need to be rewarded if they fulfil the challenges as they do involve a lot of extra effort. Cinema tickets, book tokens or attractive writing books can all be offered. Visits to a newspaper, a radio or television station, backstage theatre tours (NT and the RSC) and work shadowing or meeting people in jobs they aspire to can be exciting motivators as well as rewards for hard work. However, the most effective reward is constructive feedback and encouragement from the teacher.

Homework policy

Parents of very able pupils and, from time to time, the pupils themselves, complain about having either too much homework or too little and sometimes complaints are made about the nature of the tasks being too easy. This is particularly the case in Years 7 and 8.

To head off this kind of criticism, the department needs to discuss the benefits for able pupils of reducing the number of homework tasks per term in English and instead introducing a system of fewer – yet high quality, **engaging** – assignments to be completed over several weeks such as:

- Pupils given two to three weeks or more to prepare **in-depth** contributions to, or presentations for, a forthcoming lesson or video conference.

- Interesting, challenging assignments demanding higher order thinking (see Chapter 4).

- Assignments offering opportunities for different learning styles (see Chapter 4).

It would be very exciting indeed if this were done against a backdrop of all departments engaging in a whole-school review of the purpose and effectiveness of homework for all pupils. A programme of fewer homework tasks for all pupils in every subject has already been implemented in some schools with very successful results. Two to three assignments every term would probably be about right. Not all of these, of course, should be written tasks. Some should be aimed at developing speaking and listening skills, others, research abilities. The number of assignments would need to be adjusted to take account of school examinations and other significant events. Each subject could then focus on carefully planning appropriate tasks for different groups or some individual pupils, making modifications where necessary to address particular needs. The assignments for each subject and year group with dates for handing in could then be posted on the school website for parents and pupils to access.

If the school can also engage in creatively thinking how it can allocate staff high quality time for marking the assignments so that good quality, formative feedback can be given, so much the better. An imaginative system of rewards for really good work on these assignments would also encourage pupils to invest their best efforts rather than, as so often happens at present, dashing off a homework task on the bus or copying a friend's work.

INSET activities

The following can be used as topics for INSET at departmental meetings and on whole-school INSET days.

An excellent starting point would be for the whole department to explore the guidance on teaching gifted and talented pupils given by QCA on the website www.nc.uk.net/gt/english. There are web pages raising issues associated with teaching the most able in English and links to general guidance on teaching the gifted and talented in the context of an inclusive curriculum. There are also excellent sample ideas for English units of work for each Key Stage, activities beyond the classroom, resources, monitoring and evaluation and examples of pupils' work.

Identification issues

- Discuss the qualities teachers might look for in pupils who are particularly able in English using the ID cards (see Chapter 3).

- Discuss examples of pupils' work that demonstrate some of those qualities, e.g. subtle insight, sophisticated syntax, adventurous vocabulary, etc.

- Identify underachievers – use the Behaviour ID card (see Chapter 3) and Key Stage 2 English and CAT scores to consider who might be underachieving and possible strategies for tackling the problem.

Establishing a classroom climate in which the most able can flourish

- Draw out the characteristics of teachers who create a classroom climate in which the most able can flourish, using video clips, feedback from students, classroom observers, teachers' self-evaluation forms, extracts from books such as *Gifted Children Grown Up* by Joan Freeman (2001), and from contemporary novels or biographies.

Reading to challenge the most able

- The local library service might be able to lead a session on choosing up-to-date high quality fiction for able students.

- Each member of the department reads a book on the list of challenging modern fiction – see accompanying website – and reports back to the department.

- Discuss techniques for promoting excitement about reading.

Developing writing

Department members contribute to a resources box or a booklet for developing writing for most able pupils to include:

- examples of arresting beginnings – novels, plays, poetry

- quotations on writing by established writers

- extracts on writing by writers (Margaret Atwood's book on writing, *Negotiating With the Dead: A Writer on Writing*, and Stephen King's book *On Writing* could yield useful extracts)

- extracts on writing from English textbooks, particularly on structuring narratives

- a word bank designed to develop a more sophisticated vocabulary and understanding of characterisation.

Shakespeare

- Discuss the issues of teaching the whole text to able Key Stage 3 pupils.

- Discuss/try out a selection of ideas using a drama-centred approach to the text.

- Plan a departmental expedition to a **quality production** of the play.

Non-fiction texts

Put together a list of challenging material. (There are collections of non-fiction readily available from major education publishers.)

For any topic, be it poetry, speaking and listening, Shakespeare or writing for a particular purpose, teachers can bring lesson plans, examples of work, ideas from other schools to departmental meetings and discuss how current practice can be modified to provide more challenge and stimulation for the most able students. Creating a culture of sharing, friendly and constructive criticism, and collaboration amongst staff is the best way of supporting ongoing professional development.

CHAPTER 3

Recognising high ability and potential in English

- Identifying high ability and potential in English
- The identifying process
- Multiple intelligences
- Case studies

Identifying high ability and potential in English

It is important to assess pupils when they begin their secondary education so their differing needs can be addressed and appropriate challenge and support targeted quickly. A good identification strategy in a secondary school starts at school level and is then refined by individual departments. Many secondary schools now try to draw up an initial 'more able cohort' in the first half term of Year 7. Very often they use a variety of information to produce as accurate a picture as possible, including:

- test information, including both raw SATs scores, which give an indication of attainment, and CATs (Cognitive Ability Tests) or MidYIS, which might reveal either overall potential or strengths in verbal, numerical or non-verbal abilities

- information from parents

- feeder school recommendations

- information from agencies such as sports clubs and music schools.

The list of pupils, usually about 5–10% of the intake, is then circulated to departments who use this information and their own subject-specific assessments to identify their own more able cohort.

Although this approach ensures rapid identification and, one hopes, appropriate provision, the English department needs to be aware that many children of high potential will be missed first time round for a number of reasons. One of them is that standardised tests are not infallible.

Standardised tests

Taking CATs or MidYIS tests will identify pupils' ability in verbal reasoning **as measured by the test on the particular day it is taken**, but it is important to recognise the limitations of this kind of test for identifying ability in English. Such tests provide a useful indicator of potential but the various skills and abilities, which are developed in English, may come to light in many other ways. Allocating pupils to sets on the basis of narrow assessment will, inevitably, result in some being misplaced.

Standardised tests can, however, reveal those children who score highly but whose ability to develop sustained pieces of writing is limited. This might indicate all sorts of things and it is useful for alerting teachers to the need to monitor and investigate the possible reasons for such a high score. It might indicate a child has an excellent ability to understand but has problems with generating, developing and organising ideas and this inability to produce competent writing might have concealed the child's strength in understanding in the past. The pupil might have undiagnosed ADHD or a behavioural or emotional difficulty and never have written very much of any sustained nature, yet on these tests he/she can score highly because of his/her sophisticated vocabulary and high levels of understanding. In the past teachers and parents might not have recognised this disparity, possibly because the child was exhibiting behavioural difficulties.

CATs or similar tests can be useful when compared with other test information, such as Key Stage 2 English SATs scores. Tests also have a part to play in highlighting the potential for high performance of those pupils admitted to a school with little or no English. The Raven's Progressive Matrices is a test that does not require language (available from Harcourt Assessment: www.harcourt-uk.com). Pupils are shown a picture of a design with a piece missing. They are given several alternative pieces to fit into the space to complete the design. As the test goes on, the designs become increasingly complex and the selection of the correct missing piece more difficult. A high score on this test suggests a promising level of reasoning ability and the potential for high performance in a number of subjects. It does not necessarily indicate that a pupil will be a high performer in English but teachers should be alerted to their potential. This test has also been used successfully with very disturbed pupils who resist all reading and writing tasks. If they do well, it can be a powerful motivator as well as a clear indicator that further investigation is needed.

Transfer from Key Stage 2 to Key Stage 3 – some difficulties for the English department

Increasingly, pupils enter secondary school having already been identified by their teachers at Key Stage 1 and Key Stage 2 as being exceptionally able in one or more curriculum areas. They may have:

- been accelerated by skipping a year and joining the year group above their chronological age

- attended enrichment programmes as part of the Excellence in Cities initiative

or

- attended those run by local authorities or school clusters

- experienced special planning for their needs by their teachers in mixed ability junior school classrooms

- excelled in their Key Stage 2 test in English (with or without special planning/provision)

- been assessed as 'very able' by an educational psychologist.

All this information will need to be considered by the school gifted and talented coordinator and the English department as soon as possible after they arrive.

As well as looking out for pupils with ability that might have been overlooked, English teachers will also need to be sensitive to those who expect to be included in the most able cohort on the basis of previous school performance. If the pupil has been amongst the most able at his or her previous school, will they be amongst the most able at secondary school? The effect on pupils who have had special provision at primary level of *not* being in a cohort identified as able at their new school would clearly be a cause for concern and require sensitive handling.

The identifying process

Stage 1

A first draft of Year 7 pupils with the potential for high performance in English might be drawn up on the basis of test results and other information made available to the department. This list should be circulated to all teachers of English. Many schools insist that a code is used in mark books to indicate children who are in either the school or department more able cohort so that teachers are always reminded to have high expectations of them. These children would then be monitored during the second stage of the identifying process and their performance compared with their potential and the performance of other pupils.

Stage 2

Teachers register signs of high ability in pupils through:

- careful observation

- discussions with colleagues

- effective monitoring of pupils

- information gathering from parents.

> A pupil's high ability in English might be identified at any time during his or her school career. No matter how skilled teachers are in identifying the most able pupils, there will be some pupils who are late developers. These might be pupils who have not had the early advantages that others have enjoyed, or they might be pupils who have been overlooked for a variety of reasons. Others simply get interested and fired up later than others and begin to make huge strides.

ID cards

The indicators that should alert us to the possibility a pupil might have high potential in English are outlined below.

Characteristics demonstrated by very able pupils in English

A pupil might display only **one** of these characteristics and be worthy of consideration as being potentially very able in English:

- interested in, sensitive response to, and understanding of a range of literature and non-fictional texts

- detailed, relevant, focused responses making pertinent points supported by ample and apt evidence

- ability to see beyond the particular to the general; see connections, draw subtle inferences and make comparisons

- capacity for organising responses, feelings, ideas and thoughts in language to interest and excite a reader/listener

- a capacity for creativity; for originality, wit and vivacity in the spoken and written word

- ability to argue a point or give an opinion with clarity and conviction

- fluent and persuasive when speaking to individuals and in groups

- flexibility of approach, role, style as occasion demands

- outstanding ability to read with understanding and enthusiasm an increasing range and complexity of texts

- ability to write imaginatively, logically, accurately and clearly

- ability to handle a wide range of language in subjects across the curriculum.

Source: West Sussex Inspection and Advisory Service, The School Improvement Service. There are other similar identification aids covering very similar ground, e.g. the DfES G&T website.

It is the responsibility of the teacher to provide as wide a range of opportunities as possible to allow pupils to demonstrate their abilities.

Speaking and listening

Because of the emphasis on written responses in our public examinations, speaking and listening skills can be neglected and yet it is proficiency in these two areas that can influence every aspect of professional and social interaction. It follows that teachers of English have a duty to identify and nurture those with high ability or potential in these areas.

Poetry

Discussing poetry is a particularly good way of helping to identify pupils with high potential. Poetry's particular way of using language, its abstractness, its extensive use of symbolism, its requirement that we 'read between the lines' presents a real intellectual challenge. Some pupils will demonstrate a stamina, patience and level of sustained interest in detail beyond their years either in the discussion stages or in the writing stages or, of course, in both. The discussion element alone offers an opportunity for pupils to demonstrate ability in eight of the characteristics outlined on the ID card.

Writing about poetry also enables teachers to recognise potential in pupils whose written skills might not necessarily be accurate yet but who are showing an ability to express themselves in a lively, interesting way through the use of:

- varied syntax

- different sentence lengths

- a sophisticated vocabulary

- the conscious use of language for particular effects

- technical accuracy.

Some children with high potential might be shy and easily overlooked when the teacher is not alert to the ways in which they are demonstrating their abilities. They might have a fierce interest in everything to do with English and this is demonstrated in an anxious attention to detail, wanting to get things right even if they don't quite manage it. They might come to the teacher's attention because they are listening intently to everything that is said, clearly involved. This is, of course, the key quality of writers: the shrewd observer, the careful listener. We would not wish to overlook a Jane Austen or an Emily Brontë, both, by all accounts, spending much of their lives quietly observing and listening. Highly developed listening skills are often overlooked but the ability to listen attentively is key to effective and rapid learning. Such pupils might have considerable potential in the subject because they have the emotional intelligence (Goleman, 1994) to make rapid progress.

Reading

Pupils who 'devour' books may need guidance in extending their range of choice. The teacher's skill in recommending suitable – and perhaps increasingly challenging – books will be valuable in broadening pupils' experiences and introducing them to new genres. The opportunity to *talk* about what they have read (as opposed to writing a book review) can be highly motivating and satisfying.

Writing

Offering an opportunity to produce a sustained piece of original writing from a choice of genres – either from experience or a story – usually enables those pupils who have real flair to demonstrate their ability.

Some pupils who have been identified as being able in English at a young age sometimes seem to plateau at some point in secondary school. This might be because the child had a rich range of opportunities provided by his or her parents from an early age which enabled the child to learn to read and write early and to make quick progress. We have to be careful to make sure pupils who have shown early promise and then seem to plateau are not suffering some hindrance to their progress such as:

- undue parental pressure – which, when it occurs, can be unspoken as well as spoken

- pressure within school such as a climate that places too many demands on a pupil who has always worked hard and achieved in every subject

- peer group pressure to conform

- a desire not to appear too different from friends or peer group

- lack of stimulation and challenge in the classroom.

Other pupils who have not had early advantages can begin to show promise in English as they mature and become motivated by strong interests or goals. They might appear to be 'late developers' because their potential wasn't spotted earlier or their particular abilities were not given an opportunity to develop through appropriate provision.

Other useful ID cards

Teachers often find the following ID cards helpful in identifying able pupils in English:

Characteristics indicating creativity

The pupil:

- displays a great deal of curiosity about many things, is constantly asking questions about anything and everything

- generates a large number of ideas of solutions to problems and questions; often offers unusual ('off the wall') unique, clever responses

- is uninhibited in expressing an opinion; is sometimes radical and spirited in disagreement; is tenacious

- is a high risk taker; is adventurous and speculative

- displays a good deal of intellectual playfulness; fantasises, imagines ('I wonder what would happen if . . .'), manipulates ideas (i.e. changes, elaborates upon them); is often concerned with adapting, improving and modifying institutions, objects and systems

- displays a keen sense of humour and sees humour in situations that might not appear to be humorous to others

- is unusually aware of impulses and more open to the irrational in themselves (freer expression of feminine interest for boys, greater than usual amount of independence for girls); shows emotional sensitivity

- is sensitive to beauty; attends to aesthetic characteristics of things

- is nonconforming; accepts disorder; is not interested in details; is individualistic; does not fear being different

- criticises constructively; is unwilling to accept authoritarian pronouncements without critical examination.

Characteristics indicating possible leadership potential and highly developed social skills

The pupil:

- carries responsibility well; can be counted on to do what has been promised and usually does it well

- is self-confident with children their own age as well as with adults; seems comfortable when asked to show work to the class

- seems to be liked by classmates

- is cooperative with teacher and classmates; tends to avoid bickering and is generally easy to get along with

- can express self well; has good verbal facility and is usually understood

- adapts readily to new situations; is flexible in thought and action and does not seem disturbed when the normal routine is changed

- seems to enjoy being with other people; is sociable and prefers not to be alone

- tends to dominate when others are around; generally directs the activity in which he/she is involved

- participates in most social activities connected with school

- may excel in athletic activities; is well coordinated and enjoys all sorts of athletic games.

General characteristics

Learns easily

Original, imaginative, creative

Persistent, resourceful, self-directed

Inquisitive, sceptical

Informed in unusual areas often beyond their years

Artistic

Outstanding vocabulary, verbally fluent

Musical

Independent worker, shows or takes the initiative

Good judgement, logical

Versatile, many interests

Shows unusual insights

Shows high level of sensitivity, empathy

Has excellent sense of humour

Exhibits unusually extroverted or introverted behaviour within a group

Unusually high motivation and self expression

Speed and agility of thought and preference for verbal rather than written expression

It is very important to be aware that very able pupils might not present their abilities in obvious or acceptable ways. They may:

- have great mental and physical energy, e.g. restlessness

- sometimes show aggressive or withdrawn behaviour, perhaps due to frustration

- be unenthusiastic about work or play, or appear ungracious, uncooperative, apathetic

- be reluctant to practise skills already mastered

- be intolerant of children less able than themselves

- be tactless, hypercritical, impatient

- ask provocative questions

- demand impossible amounts of attention

- be good orally; unwilling to put anything on paper.

These behaviours might not be proof of high ability or potential but can alert teachers (and parents who might bring these to the school's attention) to question why they occur.

Multiple intelligences

IQ tests and multiple intelligences

Tests are of interest for identifying ability and potential but, as already indicated, they have their limitations. IQ tests, for instance, were developed on the assumption that intelligence is fixed and measurable. It is the 'common sense' view of intelligence which the ordinary man and woman in the street still often thinks of as 'intelligence' and is dominated by logical–mathematical thinking. Its inadequacies as a model of human intelligence have been much criticised for at least thirty years. Nevertheless, it has dominated education for decades and has had high status as one of the most desirable kinds of thinking valued in schools.

Harvard University's Howard Gardner, in *Frames of Mind* (1983), offers a different model of the nature of human intelligence, which, increasingly, many working in education have found compelling. Essentially, in this model, every person develops abilities in seven different kinds of intelligence (Gardner later added two more to those he initially identified). These are not fixed. Intelligences develop over time. An individual might have a very highly developed ability in one of these intelligences whilst the other intelligences are less well developed. For example, he or she may be extremely able mathematically but not able in his or her ability to understand others' emotions. Multiple intelligences and learning styles have some interesting and important implications for what we do in the classroom.

Gardner's multiple intelligences and pupils' learning styles: what teachers can do

Appendix 3.1 indicates how teachers can provide effectively in English so that pupils are sometimes given opportunities to work within the learning style they most enjoy and may reveal abilities that have not been recognised before.

A multiple intelligences (MI) profile is included on the website. Copies and other materials on this subject can be obtained from www.thinkingclassroom. co.uk.

Case studies

Tom – good at everything and under considerable pressure

Tom's particular strength and interest at school was in computing. When he was in the first years of secondary school his skills and understanding in this area were already exceeding those of his teachers. In addition, he was demonstrating outstanding ability in every traditionally 'academic' subject on the school curriculum. He was not, however, talented in art, music or PE. He was outstanding in English and always produced excellent work. His written work was invariably technically accurate. He had a sophisticated vocabulary which he used effectively in writing and speaking. He had a sharp understanding of challenging texts and in group discussion and in pair work he quickly identified flaws in arguments, key issues or raised the salient points at the heart of a problem. He had an incisive mind. He could write exciting, absorbing narratives, playing with different genres in a very impressive manner. Because Tom had always produced work of such a high standard, his English teacher had very high expectations of him. During Year 10 Tom broke down completely at home one day. Very concerned, his parents asked to see the deputy head teacher. She saw Tom with his parents and again he broke down in tears. Tom found breaking down in tears so 'publicly' a traumatic experience. He felt it a humiliating weakness. It transpired that he had been working very hard trying to achieve an A* in all his GCSE 'academic' subjects, trying to live up to his own, and what he felt were his teachers', expectations of him in every subject. The crisis point came when his English teacher asked him to rewrite a media piece of coursework and a twentieth-century drama piece as she didn't think they were up to what she expected he was capable of – A* standard. She gave him advice about how to improve it and he went away and re-organised the work in the light of her suggestions. After he re-submitted one of the pieces, his teacher told him that she still did not think it was good enough. It was this experience that had so destroyed his morale.

Addressing the issues

Although it is important to have high expectations of able pupils this has to be tempered with sensitivity to each child's mode of working. If a pupil is exceptionably able in all academic subjects and consistently puts every effort into his or her work, it is not helpful to 'push' too hard in a mistaken belief that this is providing 'challenge'. It is much more helpful to pupils like Tom to make it clear just how difficult it is to get an A* in English and to say that to get an A would be excellent, while to get an A* would be 'icing on the cake' – something lovely to have but not absolutely imperative to prove one's outstanding ability in English.

The importance of formative assessment (Black, 2004) is also relevant to this case study. A comment can be written praising the work's biggest strength and giving advice on an important area to improve **without a grade or mark given to the individual piece of work**. Pupils and students of all abilities have been found to be better motivated if no mark or grade has been given until the end of the year or the end of a course. In English at GCSE, for example, it might well be a more helpful strategy to award a mark based on the assessment of all the coursework pieces according to the GCSE coursework marking criteria, once they are all completed.

In addition to formative comments on work, departments might develop the use of self, peer and teacher profiling of strengths and specific aspects for improvements recorded on individual pupil profile sheets. Pilot projects in schools where pupils are engaged in this kind of 'authentic assessment' (Gardner, 1983) of what they can do show that pupils are very aware of the progress they have made, where they are at the moment and what they need to work on to develop their skills and abilities further.

For very able pupils like Tom it is helpful if English teachers can be flexible about deadlines for pieces of coursework that such pupils are obviously investing a lot of care and thought in. Asking to read what they have done so far, to see any notes or drafts, to discuss where they hope to take things from that point and then asking them when they could realistically finish it to the best of their ability, giving them an extension to that date, supports such pupils' mental well-being.

Paul – very able in English but very poor social skills

Paul and three other pupils joined a Year 9 group of able pupils for English at the beginning of the school year. At first, he was very reluctant to give in any work and invented a variety of excuses about why he didn't have the work in school completed. His teacher's attention was drawn to him because of this and because of his obviously poor interpersonal skills.

He gave the impression of being physically ill at ease, anxious about what he could do with his hands and feet. He was not confident with other pupils. When the teacher spoke to him directly, his replies could hardly be heard, he spoke so quietly.

His teacher wondered why he was reluctant to give in work. It seemed that he was very sensitive to the judgements of others. She gradually discovered various telling things about Paul. From entering secondary school he had preferred the company of adults and had sought the protection of senior members of staff. He had frequently broken down in tears in public, which he found very humiliating and which further diminished his self-esteem and made it difficult for him to face his fellow pupils. He would speak of himself in a negative way, suggesting that he was useless. His brother had a friend who came to Paul's home and kicked, pinched and punched him. He was also verbally aggressive towards him. Paul now copes by leaving the house if he can when his brother's friend visits. He chooses the company of other adults he trusts at school. He often stays after school and offers to help prepare for parents' evenings and to do anything else that might need doing. School seems to be a refuge because he even comes in on staff INSET days with offers of help.

Addressing the issues

One of the first challenges that first term for the class was to read a classic novel by Christmas and to write a report by January on their experience of reading it. Paul chose to read Dostoevsky's *Crime and Punishment*. Most of the reading would be done at home. By the second lesson he appeared to have read a good third of the novel. His teacher asked him how he was getting on with it and he replied that it was very interesting but he did find the Russian names a little confusing. After the next lesson Paul stayed behind and asked his teacher whether adults found the book difficult because another teacher in the school had seen him in the library with the book and had told him that a lot of adults found the book difficult to read. Paul told his English teacher about the conversation and said that he hadn't realised people found it difficult because he wasn't having any trouble reading it – apart from the Russian names, which he was now getting used to.

Another early task was for the class to work in small groups to discuss either Keats's 'Ode to Autumn' or Vernon Scannell's 'Autumn'. After the initial readings of the poems, when his teacher asked the class to get into groups, Paul clearly didn't know who to work with or whether anyone would want to work with him. The teacher organised one of the most able boys, Aaron, to come and sit with him and they formed a group with two voluble boys sitting behind. She made Paul the group's scribe, annotating the poem with the group's interpretations of the various images and ideas. They chose Keats's poem.

To begin with, Paul was very quiet, listening to the others and noting their ideas down, but gradually he began to get drawn into the discussion because there was an idea that he and Aaron disagreed with. A vehement discussion ensued between the two factions and the teacher was eventually appealed to for adjudication. The group was on task throughout, completely absorbed in their thinking and in their attempts to justify their ideas. Paul's unease and social awkwardness was forgotten by everybody in the group, including him.

The fact that he had been given the physical task of scribe, a task the teacher knew he could carry out efficiently, and the fact that his own thinking coincided with the most confident, most articulate person in the class, were the factors that seemed to help Paul overcome his self consciousness on this occasion.

Frequently from this point on, Paul stayed at the end of the lesson with Aaron because he wanted to add another idea to a class discussion that had had to come to an end, or he wanted to know what his teacher thought of an issue that had been raised in the class's discussion or he wanted to find the answer to something that was puzzling him. He was often interested in other people and why they behaved in particular ways. Trying to understand their peculiarities fascinated him.

Paul may never be entirely at ease socially but he is clearly beginning to benefit from the range of opportunities his teacher provides and is being accepted by others in group-driven tasks. By the end of Year 9 Paul was much less afraid of other pupils. Within that particular group of able pupils he was accepted – albeit he was a little different maybe from most people, and never really what might be called 'friends' with another pupil. It was perhaps fortunate that Aaron, the boy who is gifted orally, is also very dramatic and 'plays to the audience', succeeding in amusing them. Another pupil in this group, a girl (whom Paul 'hit it off with'), is also socially awkward and lacking in confidence. Both loved reading and both used the library as a refuge. They were already lunchtime library helpers and that link helped them to get involved in conversations about the work they were asked to do in the library.

For pupils who are very able in English but whose social skills are very poor, the following, also, are tried and tested strategies in enabling the pupil to become more skilful socially and able to work to the best of his or her ability:

- pair work – the teacher always 'gets them started' by discussing their initial ideas **first** before moving to another group to see how they are getting on

- group projects in which pupils have to work cooperatively but have an opportunity to be responsible for their own contribution, say, background context research for the *Diary of Anne Frank* in Year 9 involving an oral presentation to the class

- brainstorming – thinking collectively, say, for a character in a novel or a solution to a problem, for example, what should a school do to combat bullying?

- creating situations in which students are given plenty of positive feedback from others – the teacher and fellow pupils – following a presentation to the class which does not have to be oral. For instance, it could involve a historical and social context collage of findings, pictures, small pieces of text on important people and events which the class then evaluate verbally. To ensure the experience is a positive one, the teacher could invite the class to point out its strengths and then the teacher could ask the pupil how he or she thinks it could have been improved. The teacher would then conclude the evaluation with a lot of praise at the end.

Aaron – verbally precocious but poor writing skills

Within the first few weeks of Aaron entering the school, his teacher provided his mixed ability Year 7 class with a wide range of activities to assess their abilities in English. Aaron quickly revealed an outstanding ability to read a challenging range of fiction with understanding and enthusiasm. He also showed himself to be a very creative and lively thinker possessing a great deal of curiosity about many things. He constantly asked questions about anything and everything, and enjoyed telling jokes and using his considerable wit. He showed that he was uninhibited in expressing his opinions and spirited in disagreement. He had a theatrical manner, was clearly individualistic and independent and was not at all worried about being different. He demonstrated a lot of intellectual playfulness, pondering on how the way things are organised in life can be improved, criticising constructively. Like many creative people, he showed he was unwilling to accept authoritarian pronouncements without critically examining them first. He quickly showed an ability to argue a point, give an opinion with clarity and conviction, and see beyond the particular to the general. He saw connections and drew subtle inferences and comparisons. He was particularly talented in drama. He attended Saturday drama classes at his town's local arts centre and had been in several of their productions.

Aaron was, however, reluctant to write anything down. He delayed writing, engaging the teacher in lots of questions about the tasks. He was reluctant to hand in writing tasks, offering excuses for why he didn't have the work in school to hand in. When his teacher did eventually see his writing, it was untidy and the spelling of more difficult words was uncertain as was the correct use of capital letters, punctuation and paragraphing. The A4 paper had been folded to fit into his blazer pocket. When his teacher asked Aaron about when capital letters should be used, he was able to tell her. Aaron himself checked with the teacher that new paragraphs have to be used when moving on to a new aspect of the subject and that they needed to be indented in handwritten pieces of work. He also bemoaned the fact that handwriting was so slow and that he didn't like the appearance of his writing. He was keen to talk about the writing process and the fact that he also did not like checking through his work to see if there were any mistakes that needed correcting because he found this a laborious task. In fact, once he had written anything down, he said, he was no longer interested in it – an emotion commonly felt by writers, his teacher told him.

Addressing the issues

Aaron's teacher reassured him that he had lots of strengths in English and Drama but that, from now on, he would have a lot of opportunities to work at making his writing as effective as his verbal skills, and that he should target improving the accuracy and developing the necessary depth of his writing.

Aaron was able to audition for – and won – an important role in the school production. He was given plenty of time to work on getting his written drafts as perfect as possible. Plenty of tasks were set in Year 7 focusing on the different forms of writing – pamphlets, etc., requiring shorter pieces of writing, not always demanding a sustained development of ideas. Sometimes the tasks required pupils – or offered them the opportunity – to choose whether to use a computer.

Plenty of interactive, speaking and listening tasks were offered as follows:

- informal teacher-led class discussions

- structured group discussions

- formal debates on a controversial issue, e.g. school uniform, homework

- individual talks given to the class – book recommendations, talks on a special interest, research projects on background context to class reader

- planning and making radio programmes

- group poetry readings given to the class

- drama.

As time went on and Aaron entered Year 8 he was so talented orally that his teacher recommended he should be allowed to join the model United Nations group, until then only open to sixth form and Key Stage 4 students. He had to write speeches for the roles he took in the UN simulation days when the school took part with other schools in the region. This he did on a computer. In Year 9 he represented the school in a mock trial. This involved preparing questions and arguments based on evidence given – again using a computer. He did very well in both and was able to hold his own with students much older than himself. However, he found it quite difficult at first to ensure that he justified his points with evidence. He clearly found it easier to give expression to the words of others in drama and to 'think on his feet' when asking searching questions, criticising the ideas and arguments of others or formulating points about things read or being discussed in class.

He made friends with students in year groups above his own. Aaron was also given opportunities to attend the LA Pupil Enrichment Programme run on Saturdays for able pupils. He attended philosophy courses as well as poetry and drama courses in Years 7, 8 and 9. **All this helped build Aaron's awareness of where his strengths lay and prevented his insecurities about his written ability dominating and overshadowing his talents**. At the same time, he was supported by the fact that his teacher focused on the precise aspects of his writing that needed improving by introducing a full range of quick, 'rule of thumb' strategies to the whole class on aspects of the writing process:

- brainstorming

- mind mapping

- making spidergrams for generating ideas and then organising those ideas by numbering the points in the order in which they should be dealt with, most important first

- pros and cons columns for writing argument

- Who, What, Where, When, Why (the five W's) for newspaper reports

- seeing, hearing, smelling, tasting, touching (the five senses) for descriptive writing.

Aaron was given individual help if he needed it at different stages of the writing process: talking over his ideas, pointing out where he could elaborate a little more, give more descriptive detail, make use of different sentence lengths to sustain interest and, once a draft was finished, talking over technical errors that needed correcting. He sometimes used a Dictaphone to dictate what he wanted to write. Aaron also often used a computer but was also encouraged to practise his handwriting in preparation for exams.

The enrichment and extension opportunities out of class and the teacher's interest and support in class all helped to keep Aaron motivated and interested in his work in English. He is still conscious that his written work does not do justice to his verbal skill but he knows he is making progress, and that his strengths are recognised and appreciated and not dismissed by 'reverse halo effect' judgements about his written ability.

Matt – very bright but uninterested and underachieving

Matt never seemed interested in his English lessons even though the rest of his class was very lively and responsive. He was identified as very able in maths and he scored very highly on the quantitative element in the CAT he took in Year 8. His verbal CAT score was quite high. His English teacher noticed that his informal conversation with other pupils demonstrated sophisticated sentence structuring and an ability to develop his thinking thoroughly and animatedly. However, in group work, when he needed to be 'on task', Matt was quiet and clearly not interested in the work. He was reluctant to read when it came to reading his own choice of fiction and he spent long periods appearing to daydream, staring out of the window he liked to sit next to. He offered excuses for not completing homework and when the homework was eventually handed in it was always extremely economical, undeveloped and untidily presented.

In Year 9 he was referred to the school's G&T coordinator. When she asked him why he didn't seem interested in lessons he complained of finding it difficult to get up in the mornings and he felt as if he was dragging himself around all day. He always felt that he 'couldn't be bothered'. He had noticed that he had more energy when the sun was shining and he found it much easier to get up in the summer. By the time she saw Matt, he had talked about this with his mother and she decided to take him to the doctor's.

Matt's father and mother separated when he was in Year 7. Matt had found this particularly difficult and seemed to spend many hours of the day preoccupied with it. Matt's mother was despairing because she could not get Matt to put any effort into his work. Matt volunteered that his mother was 'always on at him' to work hard and that this had been the case ever since he could remember. He felt he was always disappointing her and that he was 'no good at English'.

Addressing the issues

His doctor suggested he might benefit from using a light box in the winter months. It seemed Matt's poor work output and lack of interest in lessons might well have been a result of the nature of his relationships at home. **High parental expectations, feeling that he could never satisfy those expectations and a genuine health issue which might have been triggered by a strong emotional response to his parents' separation seem to have had a powerful influence on Matt's ability to work effectively.**

In English, his teacher gave him a lot of encouragement and often intervened during the work he undertook in class, supporting him by talking it over, helping him to generate ideas using brainstorming, spidergrams, mind mapping techniques and writing frames, using sets of questions which would help him to build the detail to be developed in writing a story such as: What is the main character's name? How old is he/she? What does he/she look like? Find a picture of your character or draw a portrait of him/her. Where was he/she born? Where does he/she live now? Why? Who are the most important people in this character's life? Where is the narrative's action going to take place?

This last technique was particularly successful for Matt and seemed to unlock a latent creativity; he began to write a short story which developed into a very long story indeed. After he had written a twelve-page draft and it still wasn't ready by the time he was supposed to have finished it, he showed it to his teacher and asked if he could have longer. Following discussion, they agreed that he would not have to present this on paper for his National Curriculum Portfolio since he had already produced a sustained piece of writing. Matt was pleased that he had written so much and asked how he could bring it to a close without writing another twelve pages. This level of involvement in his own work was a new departure for him. His teacher photocopied the finished story for his portfolio as evidence of Matt's true ability. If a pupil experiencing difficulties produces work in draft form that is very long and this is a first successfully sustained piece of writing, it could be typed up by support staff for the portfolio and/or classroom display. Insisting that the work either be typed up or handwritten out as a 'best' piece of work might well have destroyed the rare pleasure Matt had in his own work and the fragile beginning of improved engagement in English lessons.

Matt's English teacher used similar techniques for studying Shakespeare at Key Stage 3:

- grids

- mind maps

- spidergrams

- timelines and graphs.

Using some of the tools of logical–mathematical intelligence (Gardner, 1983) appealed to Matt because this was the learning style he felt most confident in. Using these tools helped him to organise the themes and his understanding of the characterisation in a way that succeeded in actively involving him in thinking and in demonstrating his understanding about the text.

CHAPTER 4

Classroom provision

- Teaching strategies for able pupils
- Planning
- Supporting pupils' thinking
- Reading and writing
- Assessment
- Cooperative and collaborative learning techniques
- Questioning
- Accelerated learning

Every pupil, whatever their ability, is unique and has great potential. There is no typical pupil . . . no typical able pupil. Able pupils, like all pupils, show huge variations in personality, attitude, behaviour, and the nature of their attainment (and at times, underachievement). Their needs are individual. It is important for all school communities to acknowledge that more able pupils are to be found in all cultural groups, in all economic groups and across all areas of human endeavour. Definition and identification are not the central purpose of a school's work in this area. It is the provision made by a school to meet the needs of these pupils which maximises their life opportunities and minimises the chances of underachievement.

(Cheshire LA, *Identifying and Providing for Our Most Able Pupils: Gifted and Talented Guidelines*, 2004)

This chapter considers how the learning needs of able children can be provided for in the ordinary classroom as well as containing suggestions and support materials for classroom practice. The accompanying website contains lesson plans and resources, some of which are referenced in the chapter.

Many people express the view that it is difficult to provide for the most able in comprehensive schools but research by the Specialist Schools Trust shows that 'very able' comprehensive-school children, defined as those children whose results were in the top five per cent in maths and English at Key Stage 2 tests in 1999, achieved better GCSE results than those who went on to grammar schools. However, the study also found that the improvement only holds true where there are twenty or more very able pupils in the same year. There is a sharp fall-off in exam results in schools with fewer than twelve such pupils (*Observer*, 14 August 2005 page 2). Obviously, schools in this situation will need to be much more creative in how they provide for these pupils, possibly making greater use of resources beyond the school.

Guidance in thinking skills is an important aspect of teaching able pupils – so too is the encouragement of curiosity, persistence and the confidence to talk through and share ideas. Learning is underpinned by the complex and sophisticated relationships between pupils' thoughts and their use of language. Teaching which recognises this and plans to support pupils' learning through speaking and listening activities will enable all pupils to develop as critical and thoughtful writers and readers. Where pupils learn languages or think mathematically or scientifically, the processes appear to determine patterns of thought and learning styles: this can also influence learning in English. In solving problems pupils learn the ability to transfer ideas from one situation to another.

That thought precedes language is a view which has long dominated educational thinking and practice. Effective learning depends on turning those thoughts into 'conversations' to develop meaning through a dialogue that leads to understanding. These 'conversations' go beyond everyday, routine thoughts to promote creativity and reflective thinking, which requires reasoning. The best English lessons will be planned to allow this reasoned talk and reflective thinking to happen.

Teaching strategies for able pupils

Whether teaching English or any other subject, teachers need to make use of a wide range of strategies to support their most able pupils. These should include:

- a high level of subject knowledge on the part of the teacher

- sharing subject enthusiasm

- an emphasis on creative problem solving

- encouraging the growth of critical thinking

- higher order concepts and terminology in the discourse of the discipline

- a focus on meta cognition

- negotiation of learning aims/objectives

- assessment for learning through dialogue

- developing the skills for independent research

- risk-taking by both teacher and pupil

- freedom to challenge and admit error

- building on prior learning and experience

- matching the pace of teaching to the capacity of the learners

- good access to learning resources

- time to talk about learning.

Planning

Planning that is teacher-shared in the initial stage and then reflected on and evaluated is often the best form of resource. Pupil interviews and responses used for evaluation can guide and shape future lesson plans and tasks, and able pupils, in particular, will appreciate being involved in the process.

Differentiation

Teachers are well aware that differentiation by outcome is not true differentiation and that planning for the most able pupils in the classroom setting is important if these pupils are to be helped to achieve their true potential.

Planning from the framework for teaching English will comprise:

- adding breadth through delivering a wider range of texts and tasks

- accelerating the pace of learning by tackling aims/objectives earlier

- developing higher order thinking skills, e.g. analysis, synthesis and evaluation

- promoting independence

- supporting reflection and self-evaluation.

These principles underpin planning for all pupils, but they are particularly important in relation to able pupils:

- Able pupils often benefit from the opportunity to shape their own learning in unanticipated ways.

- Effective differentiation is important, as support for lower attainers can become a constraint for higher attainers.

- Able pupils benefit from tasks that are different rather than more that are similar or merely longer.

- Higher order learning skills such as analysis, synthesis and evaluation should not be left to develop incidentally; they should be planned progressively into sequences of teaching and learning.

- Progression in English is neither simple nor linear; it involves the orchestration of a range of interdependent skills with increasing sensitivity to context, audience and purpose.

Planning

Planning with aims/objectives will aid acceleration, extension and enrichment if applied in the following ways:

- Cluster the aims/objectives as able pupils can cope with more complex tasks that involve the orchestration of combinations of aims/objectives.

- Apply aims/objectives in different contexts so that pupils' skills and understanding can be developed through addressing aims/objectives in new and challenging ways.

- Increase the level of challenge by focusing on aims/objectives and demanding the application of higher order skills such as analysis and synthesis.

- Choose an aim/objective from later years where there is a clear strand of progression; aims/objectives from subsequent years can be used to accelerate progress (there is an example on the accompanying website).

- Select extension aims/objectives which go beyond the usual expectations for Key Stage 3.

- Negotiate aims/objectives by involving able pupils in deciding which aims/objectives to address in order to develop higher order skills and become independent learners.

- Encourage self-evaluation through a focus on aims/objectives that involve what has been achieved and 'next steps'.

A good planning pro forma will have references to pupils' expected achievement both within and between lessons. For instance, 'during this lesson all pupils will, most pupils will, some pupils will' and for the pupils: 'during this lesson I must, I should, I could'. By doing this, pupil needs are recognised, what is required of them is made clear and outcomes can be verified. The format on pages 52–53 exemplifies this.

When using the 'must, should, could' model, it is important to make sure that more able pupils can, on some occasions, move straight on to the more challenging tasks so that they are not always forced to do more work than other pupils rather than work of a different quality.

Media coursework

Using the covers of *Cosmopolitan* and *GQ* analyse the presentational devices used.

To what extent do the magazines reject or confirm gender stereotypes?

Use the work covered in previous lessons plus your own research to answer the following questions in your essay.

- ALL: must have a go at answering questions 1 and 2
- MOST: will answer questions 1, 2 and have a go at answering question 3
- SOME: will answer questions 1, 2, 3 and 4 in detail.

1. How do *Cosmopolitan* and *GQ* appeal to their readers?
    - In other words, how are the covers used to promote sales?
    - Make sure that you look at the central photograph on each cover; explain what they represent.
    - Don't forget use of colour, font, layout.
    - Try to show how these devices reinforce or reject stereotypes, i.e. the use of colour associated with gender.

2. In what way is language used? Is it persuasive? Do the covers offer empty promises?
    - Think about word associations and wordplay to attract the readers' attention.
    - Make sure that you cross-reference between both covers equally.
    - Make sure that you refer to gender stereotypes and explore what men and women will look for on the cover, i.e. words that suggest effort/results and time.

3. What factors will cause men and women to 'buy into' the glamour of magazine covers?
    - What are the demographics for both magazines? What is their quality of life?
    - Is it just what's on the cover that readers invest in?

4. Are we in a position to judge/stereotype people based on magazine covers?
    - Are there any ways in which stereotypes in the media can be overturned?

What grade?

Grade E

- Some focus on the text
- Attempts to analyse some ideas
- Some grasp of paragraphing but used inconsistently
- Uses some appropriate sentence structures
- Commonly used words spelt correctly

Grade D

- Clear focus on the text
- Ideas analysed in a straightforward way
- Main points organised into paragraphs
- Begins to use some specialist vocabulary
- Punctuation of sentences generally accurate

Grade C

- Good focus on the text
- Begins to explore ideas and include personal response
- Ideas organised into paragraphs and writing has a clear structure
- Varied vocabulary with specialist terms used appropriately
- Uses a range of punctuation accurately

Grade B

- Analytical ideas are supported by close reference to the text
- Coherent paragraphing
- Varied vocabulary used for effect with technical analysis
- Uses full range of sentence structures
- Accurate spelling and punctuation

Grade A

- Detailed analytical response with close reference to the text and technical analysis used is appropriate
- Writing is shaped and controlled
- Ideas expressed coherently in well-constructed paragraphs
- Uses range of grammatical constructions for effect
- Wide vocabulary and high level of technical accuracy

Grade A*

- Sophisticated response with a precise, fluent style
- Everything else needed for a Grade A

Supporting pupils' thinking

Numerous frameworks exist for building programmes and strategies for the development of thinking. One practical approach is shown in the following table, adapted from Professor Robert Fisher (1998) and illustrates how such thinking has been developed. Fisher summarises the situation as: 'The quality of our lives and of our learning depends on the quality of our thinking.' The most effective learning takes place when teaching enables pupils to understand how they learn, as well as what they learn.

Thinking	Purpose	Key questions	Examples
Concept formation	Providing definitions, classifying, making links and frameworks.	What do we think? What do we know?	Classifying information gathered through research on the internet.
Enquiry	How to observe, describe and question.	What do we want to find out? How do we find out?	Experimenting and explaining.
Reasoning	Logic and argument, deductive and inductive reasoning.	How do we know? Is it true?	Justifying and giving proof and evidence.
Translation	Comprehending, interpreting and communicating the meaning of ideas.	How do we interpret and communicate our ideas?	Pupils present their findings, through PowerPoint or whiteboard use, and explain why.
Criticism	Thinking for oneself, judging against criteria, questioning and challenging.	What do I think?	Freedom to go beyond given materials and ways of using these.
Creativity	Searching for new ideas, proposing hypotheses, viewpoints and solutions.	What other ideas are there?	Starting from the same set of information and with a shared knowledge coming up with differing thoughts and ideas.
Cooperation	Working with others, building self-esteem, empathy and respect for self and others.	What do others think?	Build in opportunities for group work on a project over a period of time.

How thinking underpins learning

The use of de Bono's Thinking Hats (1985) is a good way to get pupils to engage with different ways of thinking when applied to specific tasks. In this activity pupils are given a specific individual or group focus on the question to be answered and are told to ignore other areas of thinking. The groups then reconvene to compare their answers. This produces a realisation and understanding that there are specific and appropriate ways of thinking in order to tackle a problem.

Hat	To ponder	Hat's response
Red	What are the feelings about this idea? What do I feel at this moment? What are my emotions, hunches, intuitions about this idea?	
Yellow	What are the benefits, values and advantages in this idea? What are the logical, positive points? What are the good things about the suggestions?	
Black	What are the points of caution? What are the disadvantages? What are the potential problems? What can go wrong? What are the logical, negative points? What are the difficulties surrounding the question?	
Green	How can the idea be modified to improve it and to remove obvious faults? How can we overcome some of the difficulties that the black hat will point out? Are there alternative ways of achieving the same objective? What creative ideas do we have in this area?	
White	What facts and figures are useful for this idea? What information do I need? What information do we have?	
Blue	How have we been thinking about our thinking? Where are we now? Where are we going next? What kind of thinking should we do next?	

De Bono's thinking hats

Information about de Bono's hats can also be found on the website.

Reading and writing

Guided work in both reading and writing, where the teacher works for about 20 minutes with a selected group of around six pupils while the others work independently, is a powerful way of teaching to the specific needs of an identified group within the class and is a way of building a bridge between teacher-led and independent work. The use of guided reading within a mixed ability setting is of benefit to able pupils. Creating a parallel task for the most able within the class is one of the best forms of differentiation. These pupils could be working on a text of similar genre to the one the rest of the class is working on but with a focus that is more challenging, e.g. finding a related set of characteristics in depth. Or, whilst supporting the rest of the class, again within guided reading groups focusing on a specific theme of study, the most able group could be looking at an alternate theme of a more challenging nature or more than one theme.

The plenary, whether mid session or at the end of the lesson, is an inclusive way of sharing findings and the preparation for this presentation could be built into the guided reading work. There is a list of suggested novels for class or group reading on the website, although non-fiction texts would be equally appropriate for guided reading sessions.

Whenever lessons are planned, able pupils will need to acquire the curriculum in breadth and depth as well as pace. The breadth can be provided through enrichment by way of a broader range of content, tasks and resources. Pupils will be able to achieve a range of aims/objectives within a lesson or series of lessons and/or tackle the accessing of these in depth and in a variety of original ways through a range of appropriate or challenging writing styles. For instance, a pupil who was asked to summarise the key narrative points of a long poem was able to complete this in the style of the original poet.

Widening the material beyond the statutory national curriculum programme of study will give able pupils opportunities to acquire and display breadth. Depth of study, incorporating more detail and complexity, will challenge pupils to develop a more sophisticated, complex or abstract form of thinking. These higher order thinking and learning skills such as analysis, synthesis and evaluation will promote independence and the ability to reflect and self-evaluate. A faster pace will enable pupils to engage with more demanding material and ideas, which go beyond the Key Stage.

QCA's Key Stage 3 optional tasks

QCA's Key Stage 3 optional tasks for the more able will provide opportunities for guided work. There are three units and they are entitled:

1. Three weddings and a prize

2. The conjoined twins Jodie and Mary

3. Translations

These can be downloaded from www.qca.org.uk/qca_9108.aspx.

Assessment

When assessing able pupils' work, as with all pupils, self and peer assessment is crucial. The sharing of criteria for assessment, as mentioned previously, enables pupils to understand what is expected. Assessment for learning, where the processes are made clear to pupils and the 'what I need to do next' is explicit, enables pupil progress. Able pupils can be helped towards the Enhancing column in the SISE (School Improvement through Self Evaluation) document (Appendix 4.1), with teacher support through planning.

Exemplars which are teacher-modelled and communicated through shared reading or writing sessions enable pupils to articulate the strengths of such work and help develop critical skills and their own progress.

QCA's level descriptors provide a good starting point for assessing pupils. These enable teachers' judgements about levels of progress to be criteria referenced. The Key Stage 3 level descriptors can be downloaded from the QCA website (www.qca.org.uk).

Some general pointers for setting extension tasks for assessment

Tasks should:

- provide an intellectual challenge through the depth and breadth of the topic being taught

- provide, through the material being used, opportunities for self direction, independence of thought, leadership and enhanced communication skills

- provide an opportunity for originality and imagination to be demonstrated through problem solving, creativity, sensitivity, logic and reasoning

- provide an opportunity for collaborative ways of working, with the opportunity to discuss with other pupils and teachers.

The specific areas for the assessment of both reading and writing give teachers a clear view of and insight into which areas of reading and writing are being assessed, as do the Assessment Focuses for both.

Assessing reading

Assessment focuses for reading
AF1 use a range of strategies, including accurate decoding of text, to read for meaning
AF2 understand, describe, select or retrieve information, events or ideas from texts and use quotation and reference to text
AF3 deduce, infer or interpret information, events or ideas from texts
AF4 identify and comment on the structure and organisation of texts, including grammatical and literary features at text level
AF5 explain and comment on writers' uses of language, including grammatical and literary features at word and sentence level
AF6 identify and comment on writers' purposes and viewpoints and the overall effect of the text on the reader
AF7 relate texts to their social, cultural and historical contexts and literary tradition

Taken from QCA's *English: Assessment guidance* (www.qca.org.uk/qca_5631.aspx)

Tasks in which pupils are given opportunities to display a response to reading are often harder to find in the teaching repertoire than those for writing. When planned for they would enable pupils to display an understanding to a level which might not otherwise be attained. Assessment Focus 5, 'explain and comment on writers' use of language, including grammatical and literary features at word and sentence level' and Assessment Focus 6, 'identify and comment on writers' purposes and viewpoints and the overall effect of the text on the reader', especially when applied to both fiction and non-fiction reading, provide a targeted approach to these areas of reading assessment.

Although it is recognised that the Assessment Focuses are not hierarchical or age or ability related, those which highlight evaluation and analysis (Assessment Focuses 4–7) build on the skills in Assessment Focuses 1–3. The Assessment Focuses are appropriate in supporting able pupils when, in exploring text, readers respond to the specific aspects in Assessment Focuses 4–5, to the text as a whole in Assessment Focus 6 and then consider how the text relates to their own wider reading in Assessment Focus 7.

One way to consider teaching able pupils in a mixed ability setting and addressing the Assessment Focuses for reading is by grouping according to 'next steps', identifying the development needs of the pupils as in, for instance, Assessment Focus 6, 'identify and comment on writers' purposes and viewpoints and the overall effect of the text on the reader', and setting tasks appropriate for this whilst the others in the class are similarly grouped according to their 'next steps' learning. The exemplar class map below suggests the grouping(s) that might be appropriate in a mixed ability setting.

Struggling readers	Inexperienced readers	Competent readers
focused on early processing skills	focused on early processing skills	focused on imaginative engagement
Competent readers	Experienced readers	Fluent readers
focused on imaginative engagement	focused on interpretation	focused on literary skills

Exemplar class map: mixed ability

The following are some useful generic prompts for fluent readers, which will help them engage with and articulate what they are reading:

General questions

- What kind of book did you think this was going to be?

- Have you read any other books, stories or poems like this one?

- Would you like to read this again? Why?

- Who was telling the story?

- Were there any parts you particularly liked or disliked?

Questions about the opening

- What kind of book do you think this is going to be?

- Do you want to go on reading? Why? Why not?

- Where and when do you think this story is taking place?

Plot questions

- What happens first in the story?

- Did you guess what was going to happen at the end?

- Can you think of a different ending to the story?

- How would the rest of the story then have to be changed?

Setting and time questions

- When did the story take place?

- What makes you think that?

- Where do you think the story happened?

Character questions

- Which character did you like most?

- Which character did you like least?

- What kind of people are in the book?

- Who would you like to meet most in the book and why?

Hidden messages in the text

- Does the author use stereotypes, e.g. age, race, gender?

- Who are the most dominant characters in the book?

- What does the author like or prefer?

Questions to help discussion of non-fiction texts

- Can you think of a title for this passage?

- What was the main point of the paragraph or section?

- What facts support this choice?

- What specific vocabulary is it essential for readers to know and understand?

- Were there any details that it was assumed the reader would know?

- What questions were not answered?

Assessing writing

Assessment focuses for writing	
AF1	write imaginative, interesting and thoughtful texts
AF2	produce texts which are appropriate to task, reader and purpose
AF3	organise and present whole texts effectively, sequencing and structuring information, ideas and events
AF4	construct paragraphs and use cohesion within and between paragraphs
AF5	vary sentences for clarity, purpose and effect
AF6	write with technical accuracy of syntax and punctuation in phrases, clauses and sentences
AF7	select appropriate and effective vocabulary
AF8	use correct spelling

Taken from QCA's *English: Assessment guidance* (www.qca.org.uk/qca_5631.aspx)

Effective independent writers:

- know where they are going and where they are going to end up

- have an idea of how their writing should sound, and listen in their heads to test it out

- use their reading to inform their writing

- have a style repertoire to choose from

- attend to the needs of the reader

- rehearse and reread

- select and reject

- concentrate

- evaluate their work as they write

- improvise their own support strategies

- attend to their known weaknesses.

Some ways to improve pupils' writing are to:

- use the process of shared writing, using an overhead projector or whiteboard, taking suggestions from pupils and changing some features in response to this

- share with pupils models of writing in a variety of genres and ask them to rewrite the opening paragraph of the model, changing tense, audience, sentence style, articulating the effect that this has on the written text

- keep talking about the effect of every linguistic decision you make with a class in your shared writing and draw out ideas and suggestions from the most able in the group: this is how pupils will become more reflective and more confident in their own writing

- encourage a wide range of writing; able pupils will appreciate the challenge of writing in an alternate genre, for example a fact sheet for a specific audience rather than an essay, and will be able to determine these alternative formats themselves.

When planning for the marking and assessment of writing:

- share curricular targets with pupils (and with colleagues in other subject departments for reinforcement across the curriculum)

- target assessment and feedback for pupils to identify strengths as well as development needs

- identify group and/or individual targets

- establish personal targets for some pupils.

The target-setting process can be exemplified in many ways with a whole department (or school) based process being the most effective. The following pupil support documents are one such way for English:

Reading targets

I am aiming for Level 7 by:

- giving my personal opinion – based on evidence

- using Point, Evidence, Explanation, but not necessarily in that order – embedding quotations

- commenting on structure and layers of meaning and what they add

- revising critical terminology used to describe language and using it to describe choices made by the writer

- varying the reading strategies I use according to why I am reading

- ensuring introductions and conclusions are brief by not repeating the wording of the question

- deciding if the writer has succeeded in achieving his/her desired effect.

Writing targets

I am aiming for Level 7 by:

- ensuring I use a wide range of punctuation for effect, in particular colons and semi-colons

- experimenting with a range of sentence structures: simple, compound, complex

- maintaining the same quality of vocabulary and accuracy throughout my writing

- re-reading my work with the audience in mind – how do I want them to react?

- carrying out a peer assessment and acting on the feedback

- knowing that 'less is more' sometimes – can I edit unnecessary words and phrases?

- consistently applying the conventions of the particular text-type I am using? If I can, compare it to an example.

Although Level 8 and Exceptional Performance are no longer assessed within the Key Stage 3 tests the criteria, in Appendix 4.2, are still applicable for use in assessing able pupils' work.

Some teaching implications and suggestions for reading and writing are:

1. Focus on the text, considering the purpose and therefore potential audience and style prior to reading.

2. Reading approaches: shared reading on interactive whiteboard initially discussing meaning of text and then focusing on directed questions.

3. Demonstrate annotation of text referencing word and sentence techniques used by the writer to reflect his/her point of view.

4. Allow pupils to identify further techniques and explain/annotate these.

5. Focus on exemplars and annotate as a class, and discuss why the example is successful.

6. Demonstrate writing and then scaffold attempts by providing challenging sentence starters.

7. After pupils have written, allow paired peer assessment which is criteria based. Pupils identify three positives and one or two areas for development in the writing and explain these.

When reading a text analytically pupils can be encouraged to consider the following:

Tools for analysing texts	
Purpose	<ul><li>Why has the author decided to write the piece, e.g. shock, entertain, persuade, explain?</li><li>Who is the intended audience; who is it aimed at and what features can you select which support this?</li><li>Where might you find the text, e.g. textbook, newspaper, novel?</li></ul>
Writer's point of view	<ul><li>What is the opinion or attitude of the writer to the topic they are discussing; are they in favour, against?</li><li>What feelings or emotions do they have to the subject; anger, pleasure, horror?</li><li>Are they biased or objective/emotionally involved or impartial?</li></ul>
Content	<ul><li>What is the passage actually about? Which key ideas are involved?</li><li>What type of information has the writer chosen to select and what does this tell you about their point of view?</li></ul>

Structure of text	• In what order have the paragraphs been presented? What does this tell you about their importance?
	• How are they structured; how do arguments link together, do they link logically or not?
	• What is the introduction, conclusion; how do these impact upon the reader?
	• Are key themes, ideas, arguments repeated or do they run through text? This will link to content and writer's point of view.
Style	• What type of language is used; standard English/slang?
	• What tone is used; sarcastic, objective, aggressive, humorous?
	• What narrative voice is selected: first, second or third person? Why?
	• Is language literal or metaphoric?
	• Does the piece stick to the same tense? Language choices will depend on purpose, audience, point of view, etc.
Imagery	• Does the writer use metaphoric language; similes, metaphors, personification, alliteration, etc.?
	• What pictures or images are they creating for the reader? What impact has the feeling they are trying to convey? Does it work?
Sentence construction	• Are long or short sentences used? Why? How does this create sounds, rhythms, suspense, build terror?
	• How do sentence choices reflect the message, appeal to the target audience and reinforce the content of the article?
Impact on reader	• How is the reader supposed to feel? How does the writer manipulate the reader?
	• How do you as a reader feel; personal response?

Cooperative and collaborative learning techniques

Forms of cooperative and collaborative learning techniques have been shown to improve learning. The techniques can be used explicitly with pupils to help them develop their understanding of their learning and thereby support learning to learn. Teacher-selected groups would be the best first groupings, enabling the grouping of pupils according to the desired outcome of purpose, i.e. pupils by ability groups or a lead pupil to each group or mixed ability groups. In grouping the important question to consider is how the collaborative task will improve the pupils' opportunity to learn. It gives the opportunity for their engagement with the content to be different and for them to get better feedback from their learning. Some of the characteristics of such successful collaborative learning are:

• face to face interaction

• positive interdependence

- individual responsibility or accountability

- collaborative skills or interpersonal effectiveness

- reflection on processes as well as outcomes.

In terms of inclusion this will potentially improve all pupils' ability to learn. One of these techniques is guided reciprocal peer questioning where the aim is to generate discussion among pupil groups about a specific topic or content area. The process takes the following course:

1. The teacher conducts a brief lecture on a topic or content area for about 10 to 15 minutes. The task could also be based on a reading or writing task.

2. The teacher then gives the pupils a set of generic questions.

3. Students work individually to write their own questions based on the material being covered. Students should use as many question stems as possible.

4. Grouped into learning teams, each student offers a question for discussion, using the different stems.

Students do not have to be able to answer the questions that they pose. The activity is designed to force students to think about ideas relevant to the content area. Some sample questions are:

- What is the main idea of . . . ?

- What if . . . ?

- How does . . . affect . . . ?

- What is a new example of . . . ?

- Explain why . . .

- Explain how . . .

- How does this relate to what I have learned before?

- What conclusions can I draw about . . . ?

- What is the difference between . . . and . . . ?

- How are . . . and . . . similar?

- How would I use . . . to . . . ?

- What are the strengths and weaknesses of . . . ?

- What is the best . . . and why?

Other activities and ideas are available from:

- http://curry.edschool.virginia.edu/go/readquest/strat/rt.html

- www.jigsaw.org

- www.wcer.wisc.edu/archive/cl1/CL/doingcl/tapps.htm

- www.eazhull.org.uk/nlc/doughnut.htm

Mysteries

Another way of engaging pupils is to use the Mystery approach where pupils are given statements from a new, unknown resource, for example a novel, and are then asked to group them so that an idea of the storyline and content can be predicted. A few red herrings can be included to raise the stakes of the discussion and prediction, thereby continuing and increasing the pupils' levels of engagement and interest. The website contains an example of discussion cards relating to the mystery question, 'Was Alice bad?' to be used prior to the teaching of *Bad Alice: in the Shadow of the Red Queen* by Jean Ure (published by Hodder ISBN 0-340-88357-X).

Edward de Bono (1992) comments that everyday thought can create an 'Intelligence Trap' where pupils remain at the level of thinking that they know, rather than become open to new ideas and ways of thinking. He continues, 'We need thinking to make even better use of information.' To know how to be a good thinker, pupils need to:

- believe that they can think

- understand that thinking can be developed

- make a deliberate effort

- tackle complicated issues to make them simple

- take small steps

- separate 'you' from 'your thinking'

- aim to explore and get better ideas

- be aware that listening to learn is key

- always be humble and constructive

- consider other options and try out new ideas.

Pupils make effective gains in learning when activities require more than just acquiring knowledge for its own sake. Pupils make greatest progress when they engage in thinking to advance learning, thereby developing meaning and understanding, which is supported and assessed through the criteria for speaking and listening.

Questioning

Questioning is fundamental to good teaching and learning.

(Key Stage 3 National Strategy Pedagogy and Practice Unit 7:
Questioning, DfES 2004)

Effective questioning as part of a lesson will help ensure that pupils are more likely to:

- develop a fuller understanding of an idea because they have tried to explain it themselves

- be clear about the key issues in a lesson

- easily recall existing knowledge

- be able to link the ideas in the lesson with their existing knowledge

- tackle problems at a deep level and be able to extend their thinking

- engage easily with a task because they are clear about what is expected

- develop independence in the way they learn and think.

Questions are crucial in helping learners acquire a better understanding to solve problems, whether linguistic or otherwise. Higher-level questions require more sophisticated thinking from pupils and are central to pupils' cognitive development. Pupils' levels of achievement can be increased by regular access to higher order thinking. Questions that help pupils engage in higher order thinking skills, such as synthesis and evaluation, are most effective when pre-planned, despite the fact that questioning is characterised by instinctive practice. Whereas closed questions, having one clear answer, are useful for checking understanding during explanation and in recap sessions, open questions will help develop higher thinking skills by giving pupils the opportunity to give a range of appropriate responses. The practice of asking pupils to consider a response, for example, 'Do you agree with that point?' or 'What do you think about that idea?' will encourage pupils to engage and evaluate.

There are a number of practical tips suggested in *Key Stage 3 National Strategy Pedagogy and Practice Unit 7: Questioning* (DfES, 2004) which relate to questioning of all pupils, including able pupils:

- Be clear why you are asking the question.

- Plan sequences of questions that make increasingly challenging cognitive demands on pupils.

- Give pupils time to think of and develop an answer.

- Ask conscripts rather than volunteers to answer questions.

By employing these tactics a fully inclusive process can be achieved, with the questions chosen ensuring that all pupils are targeted where appropriate. All pupils will see that they are learning something, especially if the questioning process is explained to them and does not continue for too long. The creation of a safe environment is the key to enabling pupils to take risks when answering and explanation is one means to achieve this, together with 'wait time' and allowing pupils discussion or planning time of perhaps two or three minutes if a collaborative response is appropriate. The 'no hands rule' will enable the teacher to take responses on all levels from a range of pupils within the class, without individual pupils feeling that they are being 'picked on'. Probing can be used to move pupils' thinking on, with prompts such as 'Tell me more about that' or 'What are the other reasons for this?'

In planning for questions start with the main questions you want to ask in a particular lesson. Link these to the aims/objectives of the lesson. For instance if you are wanting to ensure that pupils can explain and justify the process of authorial technique and intent in an extract, start with Knowledge as a cognitive objective and work through to Synthesis and Evaluation. Questions at this level will challenge pupils and help them develop their thinking so that they become more effective learners. Bloom researched thousands of questions routinely asked by teachers. His findings suggest that most learning-focused questions asked in classrooms fall into the first two categories, of Knowledge and Comprehension, with few questions falling into the other categories which relate, increasingly, to higher order thinking skills.

The following chart shows the hierarchical nature of Bloom's taxonomy of educational objectives and gives examples of possible instructions which might be given to pupils at each level.

Thinking skills	
Evaluation	evaluate, give an opinion, argue, assess, defend, decide, recommend, justify, conclude
Synthesis	re-organise, arrange, propose, re-write, construct, plan, write a report, speculate, hypothesise
Analysis	analyse, classify, order, explain, connect, compare/contrast, cause/effect, fact/opinion, criticise, correlate
Application	apply, interpret, change or modify, relate
Comprehension	describe, explain, locate, select, summarise, interpret, predict
Knowledge	list, define, underline, tell, describe, identify, show, label, collect, examine, tabulate, recall, remember, find information

Bloom's taxonomy – levels of thinking

One supportive way of sharing Bloom's taxonomy with pupils is shown below. In addition, by using the taxonomies as A4 posters displayed around the classroom (as shown in Appendix 4.3), pupils can be referenced to the style of questions that they are asking or accessing. The task sheet references these as examples of prompts to encourage thoughtful responses using Bloom's taxonomy of questioning:

Levels of thinking and questioning

Clue sheet – based on 'The Speckled Band' by Sherlock Holmes

For each of the questions, match them with the correct level of questioning. Once your group has matched all 6 questions, fill in the sheet below and stick it in your sentence level exercise book.

1. Could you select one reason why you believe your sister died?

2. Your explanation about the iron bars was a little general. Could you tell me more about them?

3. In what sequence did events take place on the night Julia died?

4. What is the view from Julia's bedroom window?

5. How could you tell that there were no marks of violence on your sister?

6. How could you tell the difference between the whistle you heard and the sounds of your stepfather's wild animals?

Extension task

● Underline the keyword in each question which hints at the level of questioning.

● Then write down the keyword from the list of words underneath that level of questioning which shows what skill is being used.

Homework

1. Read the conclusion to the story 'The Speckled Band'.

2. Answer the following questions in your exercise book.

Homework questions

1. Were you surprised by the conclusion? Why or why not? Give developed reasons for your answer. Tip: Higher level answers will refer to earlier stages of the story in their response.

2. What 3 questions would you have wanted to ask Dr Roylott? Aim for a range of open and closed, as well as higher level thinking-style questions which would expect Dr Roylott to differentiate, assess, argue or predict.

3. Are there any questions that are still left unanswered? Make a list of them. If there aren't, explain whether or not you are satisfied with the conclusion.

Able pupils are well equipped to create their own questions and QUADS and KWL grids can be used to assist this (see Appendices 4.4 and 4.5). These grids are useful for all relevant forms of research, generically as well as in English, and would be best employed in the scaffolding part of the lesson.

Accelerated learning

Accelerated learning is a term often applied to a potpourri of teaching strategies designed to motivate pupils and maximise performance. The learning principles that underpin accelerated learning are:

- all meaningful learning involves risk

- pupils learn through structured challenge

- learning is about seeking and securing connections

- pupils need opportunities to reflect, ask questions and hypothesise

- learning needs reflection for consolidation and transfer.

The accelerated learning model:

- is about seeking and securing connections

- evolves through exploration, mimicry and rehearsal

- occurs when students can see the benefits of learning for themselves

- occurs when we scaffold high cognitive challenge and negotiated risk

- requires optimism about realisable learning goals

- occurs through the senses, recognising Visual, Auditory and Kinaesthetic learners

- is socially constructed with language as its medium

- thrives on immediate performance feedback and space for reflection

- benefits from a view that intelligence is complex, modifiable and multiple

- involves the active engagement of different memory systems

- requires rehearsal in a variety of situations.

In applying the accelerated model of learning there are, according to ALITE (www.alite.co.uk) four distinct phases: connection, activation, demonstration and consolidation:

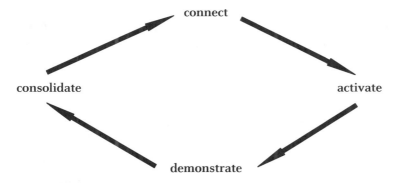

Four-stage cycle for engaging learners

In implementing accelerated learning the teacher needs to focus on the learning outcomes by asking the question, 'What will the pupils have learned and be able to do by the end of the lesson that they could not do before?' Pupils should be involved in deciding what would be a good learning outcome and the QUADS and KWL grids would be useful here. The learning should stretch pupils and relating the agreed learning outcomes to Bloom's taxonomy of thinking would ensure this. The process of distinguishing between the learning outcomes by using the descriptors 'must', 'should' and 'could' might also prove useful. The learning outcomes should help pupils access and understand the links between separate learning experiences.

To engage in the **connection phase** of learning, pupils might, for example, unscramble seven keywords from the previous lesson to solve the keyword mystery. The keywords could also be part of a word search activity with the 'found' words being ordered to give the focus of the learning. In a ranking exercise pupils are given nine statements that relate to the previous week's learning which then are prioritised into a diamond, 1,2,3,2,1. They rank against criteria. Pupils can Post-it note the three most important things they think they learned in the last lesson. These can be shared on a display board. Similarly pupils can Post-it note questions that they want answering and these can be shared and answered or can be referenced later in the series of lessons when the answers are found.

As part of the **activation phase** pupils can be given a problem to solve. This can take the form of a mystery in which pupils are given statements about, for instance, a fiction or non-fiction text which they have not encountered previously. These statements, printed on cards, are then grouped and discussed in order to provide the predictive answer to a question regarding the text. There could be a few 'untrue' or non-relevant 'red herring' statements to add a greater cognitive level to the activity. This alternative dimension might best be used after familiarisation with the mystery process to lessen the possibility of pupils' anger at being 'misled', or after a forewarning that there are some non-relevant statements. Pupils could be given examples of linguistic terms and asked to name them, unprompted. Learning could be presented in the context of a real-life situation or problem to be solved, as, for instance, in discussing controversial issues such as euthanasia or animal vivisection. The use of home and away groups where pupils start in a home group in order to develop an action plan for a project and then move into an away or expert group where they research the topic before returning to the home group to share what they have learned can be a positive and active way to develop learning. A series of carousel activities to support learning could have, for example, a tape recording of a spoken conversation, some form of visual learning and finally some form of written material for pupils to experience before embarking on the **demonstration phase**.

The ways in which pupils can demonstrate what they have learned could include explaining it to someone else, hotseating as below, as a character or object, or designing a web page with all the appropriate conventions to present their findings. A simulated press conference is a good way for pupils to share learning: they present their findings and the audience, acting as the press pack, ask questions and take notes. Pupils could also create tests for each other that they swap and complete before returning for marking and feedback, which should be evaluative. A simpler way of demonstrating, and taking little preparation, would be to ask pupils to bullet point the key learning points of the lesson.

Hotseating

Hotseating, a drama technique, is often used in English lessons and is an inclusive activity, which allows able pupils to process and articulate their learning. The teacher or pupil assumes the role of a character from a book being read in class. Once the pupil has taken the role he/she is asked questions which have to be answered in this role. This enables the teacher to assess the pupil's understanding of, for example, characters in the book. Assuming the character's perspective is a useful activity as it encourages the processing of information and thereby helps deepen understanding of the text. The type of questions asked defines the cognitive demand of hotseating. Closed questions, for example beginning with 'did you . . .?', should be avoided. The prompts below will encourage pupils to question more widely. The teacher could model the use of open questioning techniques by taking the role of questioner initially.

A 'beliefs and motivation' poster could be used to develop a deeper understanding of character development. A paired hotseating approach could first be used to develop confidence and technique, and paired groupings could create questions for use by others.

Hotseating prompts

- Who . . . ?
- Where . . . ?
- When . . . ?
- Why . . . ?
- What . . . ?
- How . . . ?

Beliefs and motivation

1. Why did you . . . ?
2. What do you think about . . . ?
3. Is it true that . . . ?
4. Are you happy with . . . ?
5. What makes you . . . ?
6. Why did you react . . . ?

Consolidation ensures a reflective process for pupils and the consideration of how the learning could be transferred and linked. This could be part of the plenary at the end of the lesson or series of lessons. In threes, one pupil describes what has been done, the second will reflect on how this was done whilst the third will suggest how the learning might be useful. Pupils could teach

each other in pairs, asking, 'What three things have you learned today that are important to you? What three processes have you used in your learning?' Then they could move to groups of four and aim to agree on five processes. Another activity would be for pupils to imagine that a visitor from an alien planet has arrived and they have to teach the visitor what they have learned, giving one benefit of their learning, three facts and five words the alien needs to know about and then, in a pair, practise teaching their list. Regular reviews of learning through short tests and 3, 2, 1 block reviews where pupils state 'one thing I already know, two questions I still want to ask, three most important things I have learned' are two other ways of consolidating learning.

Whatever methods and techniques are employed in the planning for teaching, in order to be fully inclusive, the needs of the most able in our classes require full consideration.

CHAPTER 5

Supporting the learning of more able pupils

- More able pupils with special educational needs
- The roles of mentors, teaching assistants, SENCO and the pastoral team
- School library/learning resources centre
- Links with parents

There are many reasons why some pupils with high ability in English fail to achieve their potential or need support on a short-term basis. For some we will never know what particular barrier to learning is impeding expected progress. In other cases, the reasons include:

- special educational needs of one sort or another

- an unsupportive home environment/culture

- excessive responsibilities in the home. A substantial number of children act as carers to parents or siblings

- peer pressure to appear 'cool'

- having English as an additional language. Even when pupils appear fluent in the language, serious discussion in the home may take place in another language. This could make it difficult for them to hone their English language skills

- a teacher whose style of teaching does not stimulate or who is unable to empathise with the pupil

- a school that has not succeeded in establishing a positive learning environment.

More able pupils with special educational needs

Children with a wide range of special educational needs may be very able, including those with physical or sensory disabilities as well as others with problems more often associated with high ability, such as Asperger syndrome, dyslexia and attention deficit hyperactivity disorder (ADHD). Every effort should be made to allow these pupils first to demonstrate their abilities and then to develop them as fully as possible.

ADHD

This disorder is associated with very short attention span, restlessness and impulsivity. Pupils with ADHD are likely to call out or move round the classroom inappropriately or to display other challenging behaviours that may mask very high ability. In English, the written work of some pupils with ADHD might be marred by technical inaccuracies because of their impatience with attention to detail, whilst others might have relatively high levels of technical accuracy but will not write at length because they do not see the need to do so. They can be difficult to manage in discussion or group activities because they do not conform to accepted models of behaviour.

Case study – Trevor: ADHD (Year 8)

Trevor had the highest aggregated Cognitive Abilities Test (CAT) score when he entered his comprehensive school but was described by his primary teachers as having a 'self-destruct button'. He is a bundle of contradictions. On good days he is capable of being charming and polite. Sometimes he becomes so engrossed in an activity that it is hard to draw him away from it. He loves books, especially those with detailed maps and diagrams, and likes to share what he has found out with teachers and other adults. He is a natural actor, and sings and looks like an angel.

Yet Trevor is equally capable of destroying a lesson with his extremely disruptive and increasingly dangerous behaviour. He will erupt from his chair and turn on a machine just as someone puts his or her hands near it. His science teachers have had to give up all practical lessons and lock the preparation room when he is around because he uses his intelligence and wide reading to destructive effect. He has an intense dislike of writing and rarely does class work or submits homework. In mental arithmetic he excels although he is reluctant to allow classmates many opportunities to show what they know.

For a small band of troublesome peers, he is a hero. Most other pupils laugh at his antics but find him very disturbing. They are rarely brave enough to offer criticism.

His mother will not acknowledge that there is a problem and refuses to consider medication or psychiatric help.

Strategies

- Investigate the possibility that he is dyslexic if this has not already been done.

- Agree a school-wide policy of support, and even containment.

- Prioritise what behaviour or work is to be achieved and put in place a reward system. It might be best to make no demands as far as written work or homework is concerned until the behaviour has been dealt with.

- Make opportunities for him to move round the classroom at intervals and praise him when this is done in a controlled manner.

- Work through his acting skills and through his love of books. Arrange for a teaching assistant or learning mentor to talk to him about some of the books he has read and get him to recommend books to small groups or the whole class.

- Invite his mother to sit in on some lessons where the problems are most severe and keep trying to work with her.

Asperger syndrome

This is thought to be a form of autism strongly associated with high ability in fields such as mathematics, computing, science, chess and music. Pupils with this condition have great difficulty understanding the rules of social behaviour. They may have to be taught in a rote manner about other people's emotions, how to respond to greetings, how to queue and the importance of eye contact. They need routine and can become distressed when this routine is altered. For example, they might become distressed if the desks are arranged differently in the classroom or if someone is sitting in their seat. Sometimes pupils with this condition can write very accurately but their tendency to understand on a literal level and to be confused by other people's emotions can make their work 'robotic'. *The Curious Incident of the Dog in the Night-Time* by Mark Haddon (2004) is a wonderful fictional account of the trials of a teenage boy with this condition. In the extract below, Christopher, who suffers from Asperger syndrome and is not used to travelling alone, is trying to find his mother's house in London. His pedantic style of speech and literal interpretation of other people's comments makes communication with the newsagent difficult.

> And I said, 'Where is 451c Chapter Road, London NW2 5NG?'
> And he said, 'You can either buy the A to Z or you can hop it. I'm not a walking encyclopaedia.'
> And I said, 'Is that the A to Z?' and I pointed at the book.
> And he said, 'No, it's a sodding crocodile.'
> And I said, 'Is that the A to Z?' because it wasn't a crocodile and I thought I'd heard wrongly because of his accent.

Case study – Malcolm: Asperger syndrome (Year 7)

In spite of careful liaison between the primary school and the head of Year 7, teachers were still taken by surprise when they met Malcolm. They had not appreciated that he would have to be taught many things that other children pick up by observation. For instance, he did not understand about queuing for his lunch and simply crawled between everyone's legs to get to the food.

His speech is robotic and it can be disconcerting when he does not give the expected answer but simply says whatever is in his head at the time. He does not understand tact and might say, 'That dress is old' without appreciating that this could give offence. Sometimes he becomes obsessed by a door or window and wants it opened to a particular angle. This same obsession is apparent in his written work where he can become anxious if teachers try to persuade him to set it out in a different way.

He is a very able mathematician and should reach university level in three or four years. However, he cannot cope with group work or group investigations and will become quite agitated if put into such a situation. Malcolm is also an outstanding chess player and was representing the school within a few weeks of arriving. In all other academic subjects he copes quite well in the top set although his very literal understanding of some concepts can create problems, particularly in English.

Sport is a mystery to him. He does not understand the rules and is, in any case, lumbering and ungainly. It is during these lessons that his peers are most likely to be unkind, although, on the whole, they are quite protective towards him.

Strategies

- Check with Malcolm's parent(s)/carer(s) to find out how aware he is of his condition and how it has been explained to him. Make sure all teachers are aware of this and do not approach the subject in an insensitive manner.

- Coordinate support for Malcolm across the school. One person should be responsible for monitoring him on a regular basis and dealing with any recurrent problems.

- Allow him to sit in the same place for every lesson. If changes are to be made, warn him in advance.

- Let him know in advance, using his name, when you want him to do something, e.g. 'Malcolm, in one minute you will need to pack up your books.'

- Teach any social skills he lacks in a very simple and direct way, e.g. 'When someone says "How are you?" you say, "Fine, thank you."'

- Where Malcolm finds group work distressing, he could work as part of a pair, where he has a specific task to accomplish that does not demand long periods of interaction.

- If work as part of a larger group is required, try to find a task that is important to the success of the group but which he can do mostly on his own.

- Visits to theatres and other enrichment activities will need careful planning. Someone should explain to him beforehand what to expect and how to behave. His carer or a teacher/teaching assistant who knows him well should supervise him.

- Encourage other pupils to be proud of his achievements for the school when he plays in the chess team. He could talk to a small group (or the whole class when he is more confident) about why he likes chess.

Dyslexia

The following 'facts' about dyslexia are taken from the website of Dyslexia Action (www.dyslexiaaction.org.uk):

- About 10% of the population have some form of dyslexia. About 4% are severely dyslexic, including some 375,000 schoolchildren.

- Dyslexia causes difficulties in learning to read, write and spell.

- Short-term memory, mathematics, concentration, personal organisation and sequencing may be affected.

- Dyslexia is biological in origin and tends to run in families, but environmental factors may also contribute to it.

- Dyslexia affects all kinds of people regardless of intelligence, race or social class.

Dyslexia can be particularly distressing for a child of high general ability who cannot understand why he/she is unable to acquire the basic skills that seem to come naturally to other, sometimes less able, students.

Case study – Michael: Dyslexic (Year 9)

Michael obtained a place at a boys' grammar school but has struggled ever since. He has an extensive vocabulary and always volunteers for drama productions and reporting back when working in a group. He enjoys music, art and D&T, and brings a keen imagination and wit to all these subjects. Michael prefers the company of teachers and older pupils with whom he likes to debate topical issues. His peers, on the other hand, regard him as a' bit of a wimp' as he does not enjoy sport and frequently corrects their behaviour.

After a very slow start in early childhood, Michael can now read fluently but his other problems associated with dyslexia remain. His spelling and handwriting are very poor. He finds it almost impossible to obtain information from large swathes of text. Even when the main ideas are summarised for him in bullet points, he still has difficulty revising for examinations or tests or picking out and organising the main ideas for an essay. In maths, he is criticised for the chaotic layout of his work but he finds it difficult to organise things in a way that is logical to other people. His family is very supportive and give him a lot of help with homework, so much so that teachers are sometimes misled into believing that he is coping well, until his difficulties are highlighted by his very poor performance in written exams.

Because he is so articulate, Michael is able to explain his frustrations to his teachers who are, on the whole, sympathetic. However, they are not very helpful in providing him with useful strategies.

Strategies

- Liaise with the SEN team so that the approach taken with Michael fits in with their overall support programme for the boy.

- Make sure that everyone in the department is aware of his condition.

- Allow him to prepare in advance any reading aloud you want him to do in class.

- When he is trying to get information from extended pieces of text, allow him to highlight the points he wants to remember.

- Use DART activities, such as sequencing a set of cards to help him absorb information from text (www.teachingenglish.org.uk/think/read/darts.shtml).

- Teach Michael to mind map so that he can use this skill to record information and revise if he finds this helpful.

- Encourage Michael to remember facts by making audio recordings or setting them to music.

- Make sure that homework tasks are suitable for his level of ability but are modified to allow him to succeed, e.g. give him a template of notes with keywords missing rather than asking him to make his own notes.

- Encourage him to word-process some (but not all) homework and insist on careful use of a spellchecker.

- For any topic, give him a set of keywords to refer to.

- If handwriting is poor, try to arrange for writing lessons using a cursive style.

- Use field trips, drama, debates and group activities to highlight his verbal and reporting back skills.

In English, the needs of able pupils with SEN can be catered for in the classroom generally by:

- being flexible enough to negotiate modifications to the task

- using Dictaphones or tape recordings so that the pupil can record their thoughts or develop such sustained tasks as the rest of the group is tackling through writing; these can be word-processed later – sometimes by the pupil, sometimes by a teaching assistant

- using mind maps with words, drawings, colour and symbols – a code – to record ideas

- using brainstorming and detailed spidergrams

- using writing frames with a ready-made structure – topic sentences for the beginnings of paragraphs, developing an argument or a description, *or* grids with boxes for recording different aspects, e.g. Point, Evidence, Explanation boxes in which pupils record the point they want to make about a character, the quotation to support their point and a brief comment explaining what the quotation shows about the character

- encouraging pupils to use a computer. It is important for these particular pupils to develop good computer literacy skills – this includes both good keyboard skills and the use of any available technology to enable them to organise and accomplish tasks quickly and minimise the effects of a short attention span

- including role-play as a means of expressing understanding rapidly without having to write everything down in detail. In working on a role-play task, the discussion involved between pupils in preparation helps develop understanding

- using drawings or relevant illustrations and presenting these in a variety of ways; this can be an enjoyable and useful means of demonstrating understanding

- taking photographs with a digital camera or videoing and presenting to the class – or just the teacher if confidence is very low; this can also be used to express understanding without relying on writing

- creating opportunities for bringing music of various types into the classroom as an aid to concentration when pupils are generating ideas or writing

- encouraging pupils to use music in their drama, in hotseating, in presentations on topics to the class.

The roles of mentors, teaching assistants, SENCO and the pastoral team

There are occasions when able pupils will need individual support. This could occur when they:

- are feeling under pressure

- are underachieving

- are feeling isolated

- need additional academic challenge or guidance for developing their talents

- have difficulties at home

- need career advice

- are both able and have a special educational need.

Who provides this support will depend both on the support structure in school and the nature of the problem. The special educational needs coordinator (SENCO), working alongside the departmental gifted and talented coordinator, will, of course, have a major role to play in supporting able pupils with SEN. He/she should make sure that clear, brief outlines of various conditions, taken from authoritative sources (e.g. The Royal College of Psychiatrists' website www.rcpsych.ac.uk/info), are available for all teachers as well as providing advice on what teachers can do to minimise pupils' difficulties and enable them to flourish. Similarly the school's gifted and talented coordinator may be the person to turn to if a department is finding it difficult to meet the needs of a very able student. Because of the nature of the subject and conversations that arise from certain books and topics, able pupils will often talk freely to English teachers about problems they are experiencing. Staff need to be sensitive to confidentiality issues but should seek advice from others when necessary.

Learning mentors

Learning mentors has been the most successful strand of Excellence in Cities (EiC) – the programme to raise achievement in areas where attainment is low. They work alongside teachers, helping to identify barriers to learning in young people and finding ways of tackling any problems. Some schools have appointed learning mentors who work specifically with the most able using a range of strategies to support them:

- target-setting and monitoring progress towards these targets

- teaching study skills

- raising parents' awareness of their children's abilities

- negotiating with teachers and external agencies, such as sports clubs and theatre groups, to resolve conflicting pressures

- running group sessions to raise self-esteem and help able students to cope with peer pressure

- working with other external agencies such as social services where able pupils are acting as carers

- befriending those who are finding it difficult to make relationships with other pupils and setting up 'buddy' systems

- identifying learning needs that are not being met and extracurricular activities for which there is demand amongst the most able.

Pupils welcome the opportunity to talk to someone who is not a teacher. Other schools outside EiC areas have been so impressed by the success of this programme that they have used funding from other sources (e.g. beacon status or specialist school status) to appoint learning mentors. In one case, a school with beacon status employed someone to work with pupils who had been identified as able but underachieving. She established a good relationship with these pupils, helping them to reach an understanding of how they might improve their school performance but also feeding back to teachers their frustrations (teaching style, inflexibility, irregular homework patterns, lack of suitable lunchtime activities). This two-way exchange of information benefited both pupils and teachers. Some pupils also observed that it was reassuring to know they had been noticed.

Academic mentors

Where pupils are very able and either underachieving, looking for further direction and stimulation or being 'turned off' by lack of suitable challenge, academic mentoring might be appropriate. There are several good examples of this in English departments throughout the country. In one case, exceptionally able sixth form students are involved in academic mentoring of more able pupils in English and English Literature at GCSE. They engage the younger pupils in discussions about the different texts they are studying. This gives them valuable opportunities:

- to explore and evaluate texts at a sophisticated level with appealing role models

- to 'talk literature' with successful students, who may only be a little older than themselves, but who have the ability to facilitate challenging, incisive discussion

- to focus attention on the details of the assessment criteria, helping them to be very aware of the qualities they need to demonstrate for the highest levels of achievement.

Another school identified able students who were underachieving in written English in Year 9. A group of sixth formers received training from the head of English on aspects of their written work that needed to be improved before being given a programme of work to carry out with the Year 9 pupils. This programme was delivered on a one-to-one basis with an English teacher present to offer support as and when necessary.

Yet another school in a very deprived area supported a gifted Year 10 writer by putting her in e-mail contact with a local novelist who acted as an academic mentor, reading the student's work and feeding back constructive comments and ideas.

In other places, links with nearby universities have been established and undergraduate English students mentor the exceptionally or most able studying English at Key Stage 4 and Key Stage 5. They might talk about how a particular essay could be approached, offer practical criticism, introduce students to literary movements, recommend and discuss reading, and suggest useful sources and resources. This can be inspirational to pupils with the same interests and help them to explore literature more widely.

Another academic mentoring approach might be to enlist successful students, before leaving sixth form, to act as personal mentors to the most able students at

GCSE, AS and A level, by communicating by e-mail from their universities. Able students can contact them if they have a problem or a question or just simply want to talk novels, plays and poems.

Organisations that might offer support for academic mentoring in English include the local authority G&T adviser, the local branch of University of the Third Age (a source of, amongst other things, retired journalists, editors and active writers) and local companies, many of which have policies that encourage employees to spend some time working in the community.

Teaching assistants

Many English departments are beginning to recognise the possibilities afforded by the new breed of teaching assistants in the classroom. Initially most teachers saw them as valuable in the preparation of materials or in supporting pupils who were struggling or uncooperative. However, English departments are adopting a number of strategies that enable these assistants to help improve provision for the most able. This might be:

- working with a small group of able pupils on a task set by the teacher

- supervising a larger group within the classroom while the teacher works with able groups or individuals

- becoming expert in a particular topic(s) and using this expertise with the most able pupils

- working with groups of able students outside the classroom, e.g. resource centre, library

- monitoring individual education plans (IEPs)

- seeking out and cataloguing stimulating resources

- developing an expertise in the education of the more able, attending relevant courses and working alongside the departmental gifted and talented coordinator to enhance and extend provision (LAs, like Hertfordshire, are now offering courses on gifted and talented pupils, specifically for teaching assistants: www.thegrid.org.uk)

- supporting able pupils with SEN on a one-to-one basis, focusing pupils' attention and keeping them on task through the use of careful questioning and discussion, and by using brainstorming, spidergrams, mind mapping and frames to help generate ideas.

School library/learning resources centre

It is vital for schools to develop a well-stocked and well-equipped learning resources centre (LRC) for learning in the twenty-first century. The Tomlinson

Report and the new relationship with schools in which **personalised learning** is key mark a sea change in the way schools should be organising teaching and learning for the future.

If the LRC, with the support of the English department, is to play its proper part as central to encouraging and supporting the learning of our most able pupils in English, it needs to:

- promote quality fiction, by getting it off the shelves and making it the focus of special displays in the library, e.g. 'Any School's Essential Reading List'; 'The Essential List'; 'Modern Classics'; 'Ten Books You Should Not Leave School Without Reading'; 'Every Eng. Lit. Student's Essential List'

- have pupils and students write their thoughts about a book on small brightly coloured cards and post these up all over the library to create a vibrant effect – it says, 'There are loads of readers here'

- hold competitions and treasure hunts so the LRC is associated with fun

- promote quality genre fiction, e.g. gothic fiction, science fiction, comic fiction, detective fiction, romantic fiction

- promote a really good selection of autobiographies and diaries

- build a comprehensive selection of popular anthologies of poetry like the Daisy Goodwin series; *The Nation's Favourite Poems* series; *Poems on the Underground*; First World War poets; collections by the modern 'greats' like Ted Hughes and Seamus Heaney; the modern poets represented in the GCSE, AS and A level Anthologies; the collected poems of major poets like the Metaphysicals and the Romantics – Blake, Wordsworth, Coleridge, Keats, Shelley and Byron; and the Victorian poets such as Tennyson and Browning

- make a collection of books about writers with different levels of reading challenge, e.g. the Thames and Hudson illustrated biographies series on The Brontës; Jane Austen; and D.H. Lawrence

- build a collection of books to support students' learning about the context in which texts were written

- run a reading circle for each Key Stage open to all pupils but specifically inviting the most able in English

- invite writers to one-off special events to talk about writing, publishing and the writer's life and hold question and answer sessions – consider budgeting for this out of the Literacy Strategy fund (Speaking of Books (tel. 020 8858 6616) arrange writers in schools)

- have a writer-in-residence who works with various groups of pupils but who works particularly intensively with the most able writers in school

- include attractive, picture-heavy non-fiction books at Key Stages 3 and 4 in all subjects to support the development of reading agility – the ability to read a wide variety of registers

- collect non-book resources such as DVDs, audio books and music CDs. All the great films of the twentieth century need to be there to develop film literacy, as should film versions of the texts set for Key Stage 3, GCSE, AS and A level. Educational DVDs should also be made available, including documentaries, biographies of writers' lives and movements in literature. There should also be a collection of audio books, especially those set for GCSE, AS and A level. The music CDs should span all types of music and be representative of different periods in history for background context work with literary texts. (Copyright regulations need to be observed. For educational purposes these are different from those affecting all profit-making purposes.)

- stock newspapers (and newspaper cuttings) providing a political balance, for example, the *Guardian* **and** *The Daily Telegraph* would be useful as would subject-specific magazines for broadening pupils' interests and topical knowledge. All the following are worthy of inclusion: *BBC History Magazine*; *Sight and Sound*; *Film*; *Empire*; *Time*; *Newsweek*; *The Week*; *The Spectator*; *The Economist*; *New Statesman*; *F1* (Formula One); *New Scientist*; *Scientific American*; and those directly related to English such as *English Review*; *emagazine*; and *MediaMagazine*. The *emagazine* can be bought with eLearning Credits. Students can then be given details of how to access this from school or home

- acquire a collection of the English examination specifications with marking criteria, examiners' reports and a bank of past exam papers so pupils can refer to them as and when they wish

- for the staff library there should be professional books on providing successfully for the most able. These should be both generic and subject-specific books.

The LRC should be an attractive, warm, welcoming place that pupils will enjoy coming to with areas where pupils and students can work and areas with informal seating where they can read in comfort so that the experience of reading is pleasurable. This kind of seating should be near the newspapers, magazines and the DVD and CD collections to encourage browsing. There should be plenty of computers so that pupils can move from books to the internet to word processing as their work demands. Ideally schools should work towards ensuring that pupils and students are never turned away from the library because a whole class is occupying the computers. Adequate access to computers within each subject's accommodation is desirable.

The LRC needs to work towards developing multimedia facilities offering the following facilities.

Video conferencing

This would offer opportunities to:

- video conference with students in other parts of the UK or abroad

- take part in debates, presentations and discussions with able students from other countries (bound only by time zones!). The British Council and LA advisory services might have an International Links Adviser who can help set up these activities

- interview people from all parts of the UK and other countries and use these interviews in the making of documentaries in Media Studies and in Key Stage 3 English units on context-related topics such as First and Second World War experiences or the role of women in societies

- collect examples of regional accents and dialects for use in English Language sessions.

Laptops

Pupils should be able to plug in their own laptops in the LRC. Schools are already investing in banks of laptops for students' use and soon many pupils will be able to afford their own.

Television and DVD viewing

Ideally there should be at least one television and video/DVD combination player or TV/DVD player for individual viewing of DVDs with headphones and for small groups to view as well as a wide screen television with Digibox so that TV programmes can be recorded, stored and viewed later for group or individual work.

Walkmans, Discmans and MP3 players

These should be available for listening to audio tapes and CDs. This is a particularly useful resource for able dyslexic pupils who may find it easier to get into books or revise texts using an auditory channel.

Links with parents

Departments will want to nurture strong links with parents so that there is a good understanding about how the department is trying to provide for its more able pupils and how they can be supported at home.

The department might decide to invite parents to an evening session where approaches to provision are outlined followed by discussions about how parents can best support their able child through their time at the school. Parents frequently want to be able to help their children more but are unfamiliar with current practices. Some schools have run very successful parents' evenings where they are invited to learn about thinking skills, learning styles, study skills, revision techniques, planning essays and helping pupils to evaluate internet resources. Empowering the parents can be a very effective way of supporting pupils and allowing them to develop their abilities in English.

When an exceptional student in English has very particular needs then the school's G&T coordinator and relevant English staff might draw up a draft individual education plan. A meeting with parents and student to discuss and modify this plan should then be arranged. It is important that an IEP is not forced upon an unwilling student and that its contents reflect his/her needs and wishes.

The IEP might:

- allow the student to take examinations in English early.

- consist of a programme of reading for which the student keeps a careful reading journal. Regular discussions about these books should be arranged with a teacher of English, interested parent, local writer or a student from a local university English department keen to establish links with schools.

- invite the student to run a reading or writing circle for pupils or students in their own Key Stage or in Key Stages below them.

- offer interesting drama or public speaking opportunities.

- suggest stimulating and pleasurable writing activities.

- make provision for the student to take more advanced courses such as AS English Language or English Literature, Media or Film Studies or even AS Classical Civilisation.

- allow the student to become involved in some of the activities associated with the Advanced Extension Award taken by A level English students.

- include an Open University course designed for able students in schools. These are organised under the **Open University Young Applicants in School Scheme** and are equivalent to the first year of university level study. Existing OU courses of interest to the English department looking for ways to support the exceptionally able and very committed student are: Shakespeare: An Introduction; Start Writing Essays; Start Writing Family History; Start Writing Fiction; Start Writing Plays; Start Writing Poetry; Start Writing for the Internet. These courses are free. Further details of how the courses are funded can be found in the OU YASS information pack for schools and colleges.

- deal with relatively weak aspects of their performance such as spelling or punctuation.

The department would need to follow a similar pattern with able pupils in English with learning difficulties such as dyslexia, although obviously both the SENCO and the G&T coordinator would need to be involved. An IEP would need to be drawn up clearly indicating the particular support the pupil will receive in the classroom and beyond.

Parents can themselves be a wonderful source of valuable expertise that can benefit an English department and its able students, whether it is parents who work for the media, those who write or act on an amateur basis or those who are prepared to paint scenery or make costumes for plays. Parents often lack the confidence to approach secondary schools but they are perhaps the most underused resource many schools have.

CHAPTER 6

Beyond the classroom

- School-based enrichment/study support
- Competitions
- Off-site enrichment
- Summer schools
- Masterclasses
- Links with external agencies

For able pupils, there is an overwhelming range of challenging and stimulating activities outside the classroom that a good English department can either organise or draw to pupils' attention. Such activities are invaluable because:

- they can be used to target the specific needs of pupils

- they provide opportunities to bring together pupils with similar interests

- in some cases, isolated very able pupils can work with pupils, like themselves, from other schools

- interests that can only be touched on in the classroom can sometimes be studied in depth

- pupils, who do not always work to their potential in the classroom, often reveal marked abilities in a different setting

- they can make what has been covered in the classroom appear more relevant.

School-based enrichment/study support

The history of work overload in the teaching profession has meant that it has been very difficult for teachers to launch and sustain such activities in recent years but, in many areas, the workforce initiative is having a positive effect in secondary schools. Additional support staff are enabling teachers to contemplate offering in-house enrichment programmes because they can assist with the necessary research, organisation and supervision.

A range of activities such as those indicated below directed by the department throughout the school year helps sustain pupils' interest. It signals the excitement and enthusiasm of the department and its desire to share that enthusiasm, providing role models of people who love great books, great poetry, great writing of any kind, great theatre, great films *and* great talk about all of them:

- annual school poetry competitions.

- annual school story competitions.

- a school magazine or newspaper, mostly run by the students themselves. At the outset, pupils need to be involved in discussion about appropriate content, bearing in mind the potential audience for the publication. It is usually not very fruitful, and is often 'the kiss of death', if content is censored in an autocratic way. It is often much better to work with students, air the issues involved and carefully discuss why any changes might need to be made.

- creating anthologies of pupils' and students' finest work by publishing it, for example, in a school-produced anthology of poetry and stories, is also motivating for able pupils. These might be sold to parents and friends of the school and/or copies can be put in the school's reception area for visitors to the school to browse through.

- Easter revision programmes for both English GCSE and Key Stage 3 SATs specifically for able pupils so that teaching and learning can be focused on the skills associated with high achievement in these tests. Even though QCA no longer validates Level 8 at Key Stage 3, some schools find that using QCA KS3 English Optional Tasks for the more able, either in the classroom or as part of a study support programme, helps pupils to focus on higher levels of thinking and analysis (www.qca.org.uk – then use the search facility to go to KS3: English Optional Tasks for the Most Able).

- a school debating society. In a school with a sixth form, senior students can often supervise this.

- 'Converse', a wonderful site run by Dr Sarah James at Cambridge University for students at school (and teachers) who love English can be used as part of a study support programme. There are interactive activities, such as the chance for AS and A level students to take part in practical criticism, and a range of resources and help on GCSE and A level English topics (http://aspirations.english.cam.ac.uk/converse).

- a writer-in-residence would provide inspiration for all but be particularly supportive to those with ability in this field.

Competitions

Many newspapers, television and radio programmes, magazines and special interest groups organise annual competitions that would be appropriate for groups and individual pupils with marked ability in English. Below is a very brief selection:

- The Newsday Competition (www.newsday.co.uk) – participating schools have a day in which to produce a newspaper or news website, using news story material provided by the organisers as well as undertaking their own newsgathering. Working to a deadline is a key skill. Prizes are awarded at ceremonies in the Houses of Parliament.

- The English Speaking Union (www.esu.org) organises annual School Public Speaking Competitions and the Schools Mace Debating Competition.

- The Magistrates' Mock Trials (www.citizenshipfoundation.org.uk) will be useful to teachers of history and citizenship in Years 8 and 9 but they also provide opportunities for budding reporters. Each team taking part in the main event can nominate a court reporter. After watching the trials, she/he has 14 days in which to complete a newspaper report. A prize is awarded for the best report.

- The Browning Society (www.browningsociety.org) offers annual poetry prizes to students between the ages of 9 and 19.

- The Trollope Society (www.trollopesociety.org) offers an annual prize of £1,000 to the best short story based on a prescribed Anthony Trollope novel. This is suitable for students in Key Stage 4 or 5.

- The Poetry Society (www.poetrysociety.org.uk) offers an annual Young Poets of the Year Award for young writers between the ages of 11 and 17. One of the prizes is publication of their work in a free anthology and an opportunity to take part in a week's residential course. It is possible, also, for pupils to send poems to the Society and have a critique made of it by a poet.

- The new YG&T (www.ygt.dcsf.gov.uk) is planning to run competitions and students can get into contact with other like-minded students and experts in their fields of interest.

- Film Education (www.filmeducation.org) offers, from time to time, screen-writing competitions.

- Football and other sports' clubs often provide sports writing/reporting awards. This can be particularly valuable to able boys who do not always see any value in writing.

Off-site enrichment

High quality productions such as those of the Royal Shakespeare Theatre and the National Theatre can provide memorable experiences that transform pupils' attitude to Shakespeare and other playwrights and generate a lifelong interest in the theatre. Regional theatres run a range of activities for schools. Films, properly seen on a large screen in a quality cinema, can have a similar effect.

Shakespeare's Globe Theatre on London's South Bank (www.shakespeares-globe.org) offers workshop sessions and tours of the theatre in the autumn and winter. There are also, of course, the summer open-air performances. Pupils can get a wonderful sense of what it was like to be in an Elizabethan theatre.

GCSE Poetry Live! (www.poetrylive.net) offers students a chance to see and hear some of the poets in the AQA GCSE Anthology. AS and A level students have the opportunity to hear leading figures like Germaine Greer and modern poets – whose work appears in the A level Specifications – read and talk about their work.

Visits to locations associated with writers like Keats' House in Hampstead, London; Jane Austen's house at Chawton in Hampshire; the Brontës' house at Howarth in Yorkshire; and Shakespeare's birthplace in Stratford-upon-Avon all enrich very able students' experience of the subject and deepen their interest.

Local public libraries sometimes run reading and writing activities for school-age pupils and events involving writers. LAs also run schemes.

> The West Sussex Book Awards Scheme is like a children's Booker Prize process. Children in Years 6 and 7 read ten recently published children's books, work together on discussing the books, draw up their own shortlist and eventually choose the winner. Pupils from clusters of schools from all over the county make presentations on the books and a winning author is chosen. The author is invited to an awards ceremony. This kind of scheme could be adapted in other areas by clusters of schools.

Residential drama and creative writing courses might be run from time to time by LAs, and YG&T.

Departments might also consider organising their own residential courses away from school for their most able pupils in creative writing or drama and invite a writer or actor to work with them and their pupils. Others involved in the production of writers' work from the world of book and magazine publishing, television and radio, theatre and film production could be invited to any residential experiences organised by the department to talk to pupils and students. Writing songs, journalism of various kinds, as well as writing film scripts, plays, fiction and poetry could all be the focus of different residential workshops.

> The English department in a boys' school in northern England organised a weekend residential poetry course for a group of very able Year 8 pupils. On the whole, they were not keen on poetry so a poet with a sense of humour that appealed to this age group was asked to run the programme. It was a huge success in terms of changing attitudes to poetry and getting the boys to write their own. They returned with a thick anthology of their work.

The Arvon Foundation (www.arvonfoundation.org) has run intensive residential writing courses for adults for several years, using established writers as tutors. They will organise similar residential programmes for groups of pupils. All courses are subsidised and some bursaries are available.

Summer schools

Details of summer schools, short courses and other activities for G&T students will be available from the newly formed Young, Gifted and Talented Programme (www.ygt.dcsf.gov.uk). The English department needs to work with the school's G&T coordinator to ensure that courses in their region are identified for suitable students.

The DfES has financed summer schools for pupils in Years 6 to 9 through LAs in recent years. Teachers and other educators put together bids to design and run a summer school lasting between 5 and 10 days. Many have been creative arts based. Funding, however, is coming to an end but other funding sources might begin to become available over the next few years.

Some schools organise their own English summer school, especially for pupils transferring from Year 6 to Year 7. This gives them the opportunity to pick out those with outstanding ability/potential and to start making appropriate provision and monitoring their progress.

The National Youth Theatre auditions applicants. Successful students attend relevant courses and are then eligible to audition for places in productions. These are for students in Year 10 and above. Derek Jacobi, Helen Mirren, David Suchet, Daniel Day-Lewis and Orlando Bloom are just some of the past NYT students (www.nyt.org.uk).

The English Speaking Union organises a Debating Academy, involving four days of intensive debating coaching, for about 130 14- to 18-year-olds in July (www.britishdebate.com/debateacademy).

There are many residential summer schools for pupils in Years 10 to 12 at universities throughout the country as part of the widening participation initiative. This is designed to encourage more young people to go on into higher education. To find out your regional organiser, go to www.hefce.ac.uk/widen/ summsch.

Masterclasses

Some local authorities run Saturday masterclasses.

West Sussex Pupil Enrichment Programme was set up in 1995 by Ann Bridgland (the then Adviser for Very Able Pupils). The West Sussex programme offers courses for pupils from Key Stage 1 to Key Stage 5 on subjects ranging from forensic science to introductions to Japanese and Russian. There are usually courses in writing poetry, journalism, drama, media and film.

Many universities have established links with schools, sometimes through schemes like Aimhigher and Excellence in Cities. The University of Liverpool, for instance, held workshops on set books for members of the gifted cohort in Merseyside schools. If there is currently no link with a nearby university's English department it might well be worth exploring the possibility of working together to provide masterclasses for students.

Departments might consider trying to set up masterclasses with an established writer, journalist, sports writer or actor living in the area. It might be possible for LA advisers to use their gravitas to help set up initial links. Booktrust may also be able to help through its Writing Together programme (www.booktrust.org.uk/writingtogether).

Links with external agencies

The most able in English usually find the prospect of spending time visiting the kinds of business or organisation in which they might one day work exciting and inspiring. Work shadowing a professional for a day or two is the best way of giving insight into the life they lead. Departments might consider working with their school's G&T coordinator, Connexions or the LA advisory service to try to set up links with businesses and organisations in which the abilities developed by the most able in English are key:

- newspapers
- magazines
- broadcasting companies
- video production companies
- film studios
- advertising agencies
- theatres
- the marketing, communications and publicity functions in businesses or organisations
- publishing companies
- university English departments
- law firms
- national, regional or local arts organisations/centres.

Appendices

Institutional quality standards in gifted and talented education

Generic Elements	Entry	Developing	Exemplary
	A – Effective teaching and learning strategies		
1. Identification	i. The school/college has learning conditions and systems to identify gifted and talented pupils in all year groups and an agreed definition and shared understanding of the meaning of 'gifted and talented' within its own, local and national contexts.	i. Individual pupils are screened annually against clear criteria at school/college and subject/topic level.	i. **Multiple criteria and sources of evidence** are used to identify gifts and talents, including through the use of a broad range of quantitative and qualitative data.
	ii. An **accurate record** of the identified gifted and talented population is kept and updated.	ii. The record is used to identify under-achievement and **exceptional achievement** (both within and outside the population) and to track/review pupil **progress.**	ii. The record is supported by a comprehensive monitoring, progress planning and reporting system which all staff regularly share and contribute to.
	iii. The identified gifted and talented population broadly reflects the school/college's **social and economic composition**, gender and ethnicity.	iii. **Identification** systems address issues of **multiple exceptionality** (pupils with specific gifts/talents and special educational needs).	iii. Identification processes are regularly reviewed and refreshed in the light of pupil performance and value-added data. The gifted and talented population is fully representative of the school/college's population.
Evidence			
Next steps			
2. Effective provision in the classroom	i. The school/college addresses the different needs of the gifted and talented population by providing a stimulating learning environment and by extending the teaching repertoire.	i. Teaching and learning strategies are diverse and flexible, meeting the needs of distinct pupil groups within the gifted and talented population (e.g. able underachievers, exceptionally able).	i. The school/college has established a range of methods to find out what works best in the classroom, and shares this within the school/college and with other schools and colleges.
	ii. Teaching and learning is differentiated and delivered through both individual and group activities.	ii. A range of challenging learning and teaching strategies is evident in lesson planning and delivery. **Independent learning** skills are developed.	ii. Teaching and learning are suitably challenging and varied, incorporating the breadth, depth and pace required to progress high achievement. Pupils routinely work independently and self-reliantly.

	Entry	Developing	Exemplary
	iii. Opportunities exist to extend learning through **new technologies**.	iii. The use of **new technologies** across the curriculum is focused on **personalised learning** needs.	iii. The innovative use of new technologies raises the achievement and motivation of gifted and talented pupils.
Evidence			
Next steps			
3. Standards	i. Levels of **attainment** and **achievement** for gifted and talented pupils are comparatively high in relation to the rest of the school/college population and are in line with those of similar pupils in similar schools/colleges.	i. Levels of **attainment** and **achievement** for gifted and talented pupils are broadly consistent across the gifted and talented population and above those of similar pupils in similar schools/colleges.	i. Levels of attainment and achievement for gifted and talented pupils indicate sustainability over time and are well above those of similar pupils in similar schools/colleges.
	ii. Self-evaluation indicates that gifted and talented provision is satisfactory.	ii. Self-evaluation indicates that gifted and talented provision is good.	ii. Self-evaluation indicates that gifted and talented provision is very good or excellent.
	iii. Schools/colleges' gifted and talented education programmes are explicitly linked to the achievement of SMART outcomes and these highlight improvements in pupils' attainment and achievement.		
Evidence			
Next steps			

B – Enabling curriculum entitlement and choice

	Entry	Developing	Exemplary
4. Enabling curriculum entitlement and choice	i. Curriculum organisation is flexible, with opportunities for enrichment and increasing subject/topic choice. Pupils are provided with support and guidance in making choices.	i. The curriculum offers opportunities and guidance to pupils which enable them to work beyond their age and/or phase, and across subjects or topics, according to their aptitudes and interests.	i. The curriculum offers personalised learning pathways for pupils which maximise individual potential, retain flexibility of future choices, extend well beyond test/examination requirements and result in sustained impact on pupil attainment and achievement.
Evidence			
Next steps			

Definitions for words and phrases in bold are provided in the glossary in the Quality Standards *User Guide*, available at www2.teachernet.gov.uk/gat. QS Model October 2005
© Crown Copyright 2005–2007.

Generic Elements	Entry	Developing	Exemplary
5. Assessment for learning	i. Processes of data analysis and pupil assessment are employed throughout the school/college to plan learning for gifted and talented pupils.	i. Routine progress reviews, using both qualitative and quantitative data, make effective use of prior, predictive and value-added attainment data to plan for progression in pupils' learning.	i. Assessment data are used by teachers and across the school/college to ensure challenge and sustained progression in individual pupils' learning.
	ii. Dialogue with pupils provides focused feedback which is used to plan future learning.	ii. Systematic oral and written feedback helps pupils to set challenging curricular targets.	ii. Formative assessment and individual target setting combine to maximise and celebrate pupils' achievements.
	iii. Self and peer assessment, based on clear understanding of criteria, are used to increase pupils' responsibility for learning.	iii. Pupils reflect on their own skill development and are involved in the design of their own targets and tasks.	iii. Classroom practice regularly requires pupils to reflect on their own progress against targets, and engage in the direction of their own learning.
Evidence			
Next steps			
6. Transfer and transition	i. Shared processes, using agreed criteria, are in place to ensure the productive transfer of information from one setting to another (i.e. from class to class, year to year and school/college to school/college).	i. Transfer information concerning gifted and talented pupils, including parental input, informs targets for pupils to ensure progress in learning. Particular attention is given to including new admissions.	i. Transfer data concerning gifted and talented pupils are used to inform planning of teaching and learning at subject/aspect/topic and individual pupil level, and to ensure progression according to ability rather than age or phase.
Evidence			
Next steps			

D – School/college organisation

Generic Elements	Entry	Developing	Exemplary
7. Leadership	i. A named member of the governing body, senior management team and the lead professional responsible for gifted and talented education have clearly directed responsibilities for motivating and driving gifted and talented provision. The head teacher actively champions gifted and talented provision.	i. Responsibility for gifted and talented provision is distributed, and evaluation of its impact shared, at all levels in the school/college. Staff subscribe to policy at all levels. Governors play a significant supportive and evaluative role.	i. Organisational structures, communication channels and the deployment of staff (e.g. workforce remodelling) are flexible and creative in supporting the delivery of personalised learning. Governors take a lead in celebrating achievements of gifted and talented pupils.
Evidence			
Next steps			

8. Policy	i. The gifted and talented policy is integral to the school/college's inclusion agenda and approach to personalised learning, feeds into and from the single school/college improvement plan and is consistent with other policies.	i. The policy directs and reflects best practice in the school/college, is regularly reviewed and is clearly linked to other policy documentation.	i. The policy includes input from the whole-school/college community and is regularly refreshed in the light of innovative national and international practice.
Evidence			
Next steps			
9. School/college ethos and pastoral care	i. The school/college sets high expectations, recognises achievement and celebrates the successes of all its pupils.	i. The school/college fosters an environment which promotes positive behaviour for learning. Pupils are listened to and their views taken into account.	i. An ethos of ambition and achievement is agreed and shared by the whole school/college community. Success across a wide range of abilities is celebrated.
	ii. The school/college identifies and addresses the particular social and emotional needs of gifted and talented pupils in consultation with pupils, parents and carers.	ii. Strategies exist to counteract bullying and any adverse effects of social and curriculum pressures. Specific support for able underachievers and pupils from different cultures and social backgrounds is available and accessible.	ii. The school/college places equal emphasis on high achievement and emotional well being, underpinned by programmes of support personalised to the needs of gifted and talented pupils. There are opportunities for pupils to use their gifts to benefit other pupils and the wider community.
Evidence			
Next steps			
10. Staff development	i. Staff have received professional development in meeting the needs of gifted and talented pupils.	i. The induction programme for new staff addresses gifted and talented issues, both at whole school/college and specific subject/aspect level.	i. There is ongoing audit of staff needs and an appropriate range of professional development in gifted and talented education. Professional development is informed by research and collaboration within and beyond the school/college.

Definitions for words and phrases in bold are provided in the glossary in the Quality Standards *User Guide*, available at www2.teachernet.gov.uk/gat. QS Model October 2005
© Crown Copyright 2005–2007

Generic Elements	Entry	Developing	Exemplary
	ii. The lead professional responsible for gifted and talented education has received appropriate professional development.	ii. Subject/aspect and phase leaders have received specific professional development in meeting the needs of gifted and talented pupils.	ii. Priorities for the development of gifted and talented provision are included within a professional development entitlement for all staff and are monitored through performance management processes.
Evidence			
Next steps			
11. Resources	i. Provision for gifted and talented pupils is supported by appropriate budgets and resources.	i. Allocated resources include school/college based and nationally available resources, and these have a significant and measurable impact on the progress that pupils make and their attitudes to learning.	i. Resources are used to stimulate innovative and experimental practice, which is shared throughout the school/college and which are regularly reviewed for impact and best value.
Evidence			
Next steps			
12. Monitoring and evaluation	i. Subject and phase audits focus on the quality of teaching and learning for gifted and talented pupils. Whole school/college targets are set using prior attainment data.	i. Performance against targets (including at pupil level) is regularly reviewed. Targets include qualitative pastoral and curriculum outcomes as well as numerical data.	i. Performance against targets is rigorously evaluated against clear criteria. Qualitative and quantitative outcomes inform whole-school/college self-evaluation processes.
	ii. Elements of provision are planned against clear objectives within effective whole-school self-evaluation processes.	ii. All elements, including non-academic aspects of gifted and talented provision, are planned to clear objectives and are subjected to detailed evaluation.	ii. The school/college examines and challenges its own provision to inform development of further experimental and innovative practice in collaboration with other schools/colleges.
Evidence			
Next steps			

E – Strong partnerships beyond the school

	Entry	Developing	Exemplary
13. Engaging with the community, families and beyond	i. Parents/carers are aware of the school's/college's policy on gifted and talented provision, contribute to its identification processes and are kept informed of developments in gifted and talented provision, including through the School Profile. ii. The school/college shares good practice and has some collaborative provision with other schools, colleges and the wider community.	i. Progression of gifted and talented pupils is enhanced by home-school/college partnerships. There are strategies to engage and support hard-to-reach parents/carers. ii. A coherent strategy for networking with other schools, colleges and local community organisations extends and enriches provision.	i. Parents/carers are actively engaged in extending provision. Support for gifted and talented provision is integrated with other children's services (e.g. Sure Start, EAL, traveller, refugee, LAC Services). ii. There is strong emphasis on collaborative and innovative working with other schools/colleges which impacts on quality of provision locally, regionally and nationally.
Evidence			
Next steps			
14. Learning beyond the classroom	i. There are opportunities for pupils to learn beyond the school/college day and site (extended hours and out-of-school activities). ii. Pupils participate in dedicated gifted and talented activities (e.g. summer schools) and their participation is recorded.	i. A coherent programme of enrichment and extension activities (through extended hours and out-of-school activities) complements teaching and learning and helps identify pupils' latent gifts and talents. ii. Local and national provision helps meet individual pupils' learning needs, e.g. NAGTY membership, accessing outreach, local enrichment programmes.	i. Innovative models of learning beyond the classroom are developed in collaboration with local and national schools/colleges to further enhance teaching and learning. ii. Coherent strategies are used to direct and develop individual expert performance via external agencies, e.g. HE/FE links, online support, and local/regional/national programmes.
Evidence			
Next steps			

Definitions for words and phrases in bold are provided in the glossary in the Quality Standards *User Guide*, available at www2.teachernet.gov.uk/gat. QS Model October 2005

© Crown Copyright 2005–2007.

School policy statement for the provision of gifted and talented pupils

Rationale

The school will be continuing to develop its provision for gifted and talented pupils during the course of the school year. We believe that our prime task is to create a curriculum of opportunity; this means creating the most appropriate learning environment so that all our pupils are able to progress as far as they can. To achieve this we aim to create the widest possible variety of learning opportunities which recognise the different individual learning needs of all our pupils: different learning rates, different learning styles, different interests and different abilities.

Developing provision for our gifted and talented pupils is an important aspect of our provision to meet the needs of all our pupils.

Aims

We aim to ensure the following provision for the gifted and talented pupils in our care:

- Access to a range of learning opportunities appropriate to their needs.

- Opportunities to work at higher cognitive levels.

- Opportunities to develop specific skills, talents or intellectual abilities.

- A concern for the development of the whole child: social, moral and spiritual as well as intellectual.

Definitions

Who exactly are we referring to when we refer to 'gifted and talented' pupils?

- The term 'gifted' refers to pupils who are very able in school 'academic' subjects. 'Talented' refers to pupils who show special ability in PE, Sport, Drama, Art, Music and Design Technology subjects.

- Each department in the school is working towards identifying its 10–20% most able pupils.

- Departments will identify any pupils in their most able 10–20% who are in the top 5% nationally.

General overall approach

Most subject departments set pupils according to ability in their subject and are continuing to develop plans for the provision of a challenging and stimulating range of learning opportunities appropriate to the needs of pupils in each set, paying particular attention to developing plans for the promotion of higher order thinking skills: analysis, synthesis and evaluation.

In subjects where pupils are not taught in sets, departments are continuing to develop a range of appropriate strategies to ensure able pupils have opportunities for analysis, synthesis and evaluation. This will be provided through developing the management of classroom activities and the range of assignments pupils are set.

Identification and monitoring

Departments will identify the G&T pupils in their subject using the following strategies:

- considering primary school comments/judgements on pupils' work when these are available

- considering Key Stage 2 test results

- taking pupils' CAT results into consideration

- considering parental comments

- checking these possible sources against teacher observations of the pupil's work and behaviour since arriving at this school and using the agreed department ID card setting out the qualities/characteristics G&T pupils might present to assist in verifying judgements.

Departments will identify G&T pupils in Year 7 and pass on their judgements to the G&T coordinator by January each year. The departmentally agreed ID cards will be used by teachers to help them form their judgements. Departments will review who the G&T pupils are in their subject (all year groups) in June/July each year, taking into consideration work patterns and achievements throughout the year and examination results. To ensure the emotional, moral, spiritual and intellectual spheres are developing in our G&T pupils, the progress of pupils will be monitored by departments, heads of house and tutors through the existing system of regular reporting of effort and achievement grades.

The monitoring of pupils' progress on the register will be carried out yearly following each year group's school or national examinations by all subject staff, heads of department, heads of house and the pupils' form tutors through existing departmental, house, heads of department and heads of house meetings. Any G&T pupils causing concern will be referred to the G&T coordinator who will discuss any necessary course of action with the head of teaching and learning. Any concerns about individual pupils will be referred to the G&T coordinator at any time of the year, as they arise. The G&T coordinator will meet the pupil, liaise with relevant staff and parents, and arrange a course of action, e.g. set individual challenges, draw up an individual education plan, consult a range of support services if judged appropriate.

In-class approach

Within the classroom, subject teachers will develop the following strategies to ensure pupils' progress:

- differentiated tasks, where appropriate, to include activities which will encourage the development of higher order thinking skills: analysis, hypothesis, synthesis and evaluation

- differentiated extension/homework tasks, where appropriate, to include activities which will encourage the development of higher order thinking skills: analysis, hypothesis, synthesis and evaluation

- variety of tasks offering choice and negotiation with individual pupils as to which tasks match their interests, aptitudes or will extend/develop them

- opportunities for small groups of like-ability pupils to work together on a range of different aspects of a topic

- opportunities for individual G&T pupils to pursue their own interests in the subject

- key questions designed to encourage analysis, hypothesis, synthesis and evaluation.

Ensuring pupil progress will also be developed through:

- teacher interventions: In group and pair discussion work, in role-play, during the reflection and writing process with individual pupils, techniques being developed by teachers will promote the development of analysis, synthesis and evaluation

- teacher feedback on pupils' work designed to challenge and extend: verbal and written (teachers' marking).

Teacher feedback will establish a dialogue with pupils through posing questions, giving prompts for lines of inquiry, presenting a counter view to the pupil's, challenging a pupil's premise, or making suggestions for further development of thought on a topic, reading, etc.

Out-of-class activities

A range of enrichment, challenge and support activities will be developed:

- local authority pupil enrichment courses

- special in-school and out-of-school events, e.g. poetry, music and drama workshops, school productions and concerts, science fairs, maths masterclasses, Model United Nations, Duke of Edinburgh Award, Royal Society Lectures, student conferences

- a wide range of extracurricular music and sports opportunities

- extension classes for able GCSE and A level students in some subjects

- departmentally run clubs and teams

- mentoring.

Responsibility for coordination and monitoring of progress

The provision of whole-school strategies and the monitoring of G&T pupil progress will be coordinated by the G&T coordinator, reporting to the SLT head of teaching and learning. All subject teachers, heads of department, heads of house and form tutors will be involved in a review of the intellectual and social development of pupils on the school register of G&T pupils through departmental and house meetings, heads of department and heads of house meetings.

Process for review and development

The school's developing provision will be reviewed in June/July as follows:

- Staff will keep the G&T coordinator informed of developments in their subject for the provision of G&T pupils.

- The G&T coordinator attends local authority meetings for G&T coordinators and will consider the ideas for development disseminated at these meetings.

- The G&T Think Tank meetings will discuss new developments in departments' and whole-school provision for G&T pupils and will generate ideas for future development.

- An audit of the provision for access to a range of learning opportunities appropriate to the needs of able pupils will usually be carried out annually, and the provision compared with audits carried out in previous years.

- Departmental schemes of work will also be reviewed for the provision of opportunities for work at higher cognitive levels by heads of department as part of their monitoring processes.

- Opportunities to develop our G&T pupils' specific skills, talents and intellectual abilities will be identified through the existing process of departmental monitoring of schemes of work and pupils' work, and through teacher feedback and regular audits – all of which will be coordinated by the G&T coordinator.

- By these means, an evaluation of current provision will be made and strategies formulated for future development.

Use of outside agencies for training and provision

- Pupils will be nominated by subject staff for a wide variety of local authority pupil enrichment courses which are offered each term.

- The local authority runs a range of subject-specific courses on teaching G&T pupils, and on more general issues associated with G&T pupils. Staff have opportunities to attend these courses and can apply in the usual way.

From *Meeting the Needs of Your Most Able Pupils: English*, Routledge 2007

English department gifted and talented pupils policy

The English department's policy for gifted and talented pupils has been developed within the context of the whole-school policy for the provision of gifted and talented pupils.

Rationale

The department recognises the need to provide for the whole ability range. Developing the provision for the particular needs of gifted and talented pupils is an important part of our provision for the needs of all our pupils.

Aims

We aim to ensure the gifted and talented pupils in our care have:

- access to a range of learning opportunities appropriate to their needs
- opportunities to work at higher cognitive levels
- opportunities to develop their specific skills, talents or intellectual abilities
- opportunities to develop socially, morally and spiritually as well as intellectually.

Identification and monitoring

Teachers will identify the gifted and talented pupils in their care using the following strategies:

- considering previous schools' comments/judgements on pupils' work
- considering Key Stage 2 test results
- considering parental comments
- checking these possible sources against teacher observations of the pupil's work in class and behaviour at this school and using the agreed departmental ID card setting out the qualities/characteristics G&T pupils might present to assist in verifying judgements
- internal assessments
- external assessments.

One, some or all of the following are considered to be an indication of potentially high ability in English:

- interested in, sensitive response to, and understanding of, a range of literature and non-fictional texts

- detailed, relevant, focused responses making pertinent points supported by ample and apt evidence

- ability to see beyond the particular to the general; see connections, draw subtle inferences and make comparisons

- capacity for organising responses, feelings, ideas and thoughts in language to interest and excite the reader/listener

- capacity for creativity, originality, wit and vivacity in the spoken and written word

- ability to argue a point or give an opinion with clarity and conviction

- fluent and persuasive when speaking to individuals and in groups

- flexibility of approach, role, style as occasion demands

- outstanding ability to read, with understanding and enthusiasm, an increasing range and complexity of texts

- ability to write imaginatively, logically, accurately and clearly

- ability to handle a wide range of language in a variety of contexts.

Teachers will also be aware of behavioural indicators that can include:

- aggressive or withdrawn behaviour, often due to frustration

- reluctance to practise skills already mastered

- demanding impossible amounts of attention

- displaying good oral skills, but unwilling to put anything down on paper

- lack of enthusiasm about work, appearing to be ungracious, uncooperative or apathetic

- asking provocative questions

- intolerant of pupils less able than themselves.

The school's register of G&T pupils is reviewed at the end of each academic year, taking into consideration work patterns and achievements throughout the year, but teachers may add pupils to the register at any time by informing the school's G&T coordinator.

- The department will **identify** pupils in Year 7 who should be placed on the school's G&T register by January/February each year. The department will supply a list of these pupils to the school's G&T coordinator.

- The department will **review** who the G&T pupils are in English (all year groups) in June/July each year and will add pupils to, or remove pupils from, the register.

- The department will **monitor** the progress of pupils on the register at the above times of year and inform the G&T coordinator of any particular concerns about pupils' progress.

At the beginning of the academic year, when the school's G&T register is finalised, teachers will familiarise themselves with the register ensuring that they know which pupils in their groups are on the register for English. They will **plan** and **use appropriate teaching strategies** for these pupils.

From *Meeting the Needs of Your Most Able Pupils: English*, Routledge 2007

Departmental checklist and action plan

Provision for the most able pupils in English

	Yes/No/In progress	Priority for action
1. Has the department developed a policy on its provision for the more able?		
2. Does it have a more able/G&T coordinator or representative who liaises directly with the school more able/G&T coordinator?		
3. Are the more able students clearly identified in subject registers?		
4. Has the department identified CPD requirements in relation to more able pupils?		
5. Has the department agreed the strategies it will use to provide suitable pace, depth and breadth for the most able?		
6. Does the department have an agreed approach to providing for the exceptional child whose needs might not easily be met in the ordinary classroom?		
7. Does short-term planning outline expectations for the most able and any extended/modified tasks for them?		
8. Are there suitable resources for the most able?		
9. Is homework used to extend the most able?		
10. Do the most able have plenty of opportunities to develop as independent learners?		
11. Are different learning styles taken into account when planning for and assessing the most able?		
12. Do you keep a portfolio of outstanding work in your department?		
13. Is provision for the most able regularly discussed at departmental meetings?		
14. Do you share good practice in more able provision with other departments or schools?		
15. Is the progress of your most able students effectively monitored?		

Stage 2

Highlight all areas where achievement or provision in your department is lacking. Decide on about three priorities to raise standards or improve provision for your most able and draw up an action plan making it clear:

- What your success criteria are or what you hope to achieve

- What action will be taken

- When the action will be taken and by whom

- Where you will go for help

- What resources you need

- How you will monitor your progress

- What your deadline is for assessing your success.

Departmental action plan for improving provision for the most able

Priority	Success criteria	Actions	When?	By whom?	Resources/Support agencies
1.					
					Review Date
2.					
					Review Date
3.					
					Review Date

From *Meeting the Needs of Your Most Able Pupils: English*, Routledge 2007

Multiple intelligences table

Intelligence	What is it?	Pupils like to	Teachers can
Interpersonal	• sensitive to the feelings and moods of others • understand and interact effectively with others	• enjoy friends • lead and share ideas • build agreement and empathise with others • work as an effective team member	• set up pair/group activities • class/group/pair brainstorm solutions to problems • set up situations in which pupils are given feedback from others
Intrapersonal	• sensitive to one's own feelings and moods • know own strengths and weaknesses • use self-knowledge to influence decisions and personal aspirations	• control own feelings and moods • pursue personal interests and set personal agendas • learn through observing and listening • have time to reflect	• enable pupils to work at own pace • set up individual, self-directed projects • help pupils set aspirations • provide opportunities for pupils to get feedback from each other • involve pupils in journal writing, making a commonplace book and other writing tasks offering reflection
Bodily–kinaesthetic	• use one's body to communicate and solve problems • is skilful with objects and activities involving motor skills	• play sport and be physically active • use body language • do crafts and make things • dance, act or mime	• offer role-playing and acting opportunities • involve pupils in physical activity whenever possible • set up tasks that allow the students to move while working
Linguistic	• think in words • use language and words in many different forms to express complex meanings	• read, write or tell stories • use an adventurous vocabulary • create poems and stories using the sounds and imagery of words • tell jokes, riddles or use puns • play word games	• set up the full range of speaking and listening, reading and writing activities to be found in the secondary English subject specialist's classroom
Logical–mathematical	• approach problems logically • understand number and abstract patterns • recognise and solve problems using reasoning skills	• work with numbers, work things out and analyse situations • know how things work • ask questions • demonstrate precision in problem solving	• get pupils to make timelines, make maps, graphs, pie charts, etc.

Intelligence	What is it?	Pupils like to	Teachers can
		• work in situations in which there are clear black-and-white solutions	
Musical	• sensitive to non-verbal sounds in the environment • aware of patterns in rhythm	• listen to and play music • match emotions to music and rhythms • sing, hum and move to music • remember and work with different musical forms • create and replicate tunes	• rewrite song lyrics to teach a concept • encourage pupils to add music to drama • create musical mnemonics • teach literature through music of the period and/or place, e.g. 'Poems From Other Cultures' (AQA GCSE)
Naturalist	• sensitive to the natural world • sees connections and patterns in the plant and animal worlds	• spend time outdoors • observe plants and animals, collect rocks, try to catch animals • listen to the sounds created in the natural world • notice relationships in nature • categorise and classify flowers and animals	• use the outdoors as a classroom • think of opportunities to bring natural objects into the English classroom, e.g. frogspawn for Heaney's 'Death of a Naturalist', Autumn leaves, acorns etc. for Autumn poems, blackberries for Heaney's 'Blackberry Picking'
Spatial	• perceive the visual world accurately • create mental images • think three-dimensionally • aware of relationship between objects in space	• doodle, paint, draw or create three-dimensional representations • look at maps • work at puzzles or mazes • take things apart and put them back together	• think of opportunities for drawing maps when using literary and other texts, e.g. plotting pilgrims' journey to Canterbury when working on *The Canterbury Tales* • provide opportunities to show understanding through art work • get pupils to design clothing and sets in drama work or work with plays

 From *Meeting the Needs of Your Most Able Pupils: English*, Routledge 2007

Pupil teaching and learning – SISE document

Key Area		Focusing	Developing	Establishing	Enhancing
Objective-led lessons	Pupils	*Pupils are unaware of lesson objectives but...* In some lessons pupils are able to explain what they are learning and the purpose of the task, although this is not routine.	Pupils, when asked, are beginning to be able to explain the objective of their work, although sometimes lack the specific language to explain it in the context of the subject.	With some guidance pupils are increasingly able to understand what they are doing, how well they are doing and what they need to do to improve.	Pupils record the learning objective as part of their work and are confident to either orally or in written form review progress against the learning objective.
		Pupils have little appreciation of their achievements and lack awareness of predetermined criteria.	*Pupils have some appreciation of achievement but have no support to link this to success criteria.*	Pupils, when supported, are able to determine their achievements against predetermined criteria.	Pupils are aware of a range of learning outcomes and are able to determine their achievements in relation to criteria.
		Pupils are content with their current level of achievement.	*Pupils are aware of the need to improve but lack the guidance to progress.*	*With some guidance pupils are increasingly able to understand what they need to do to improve.*	Pupils are able to independently identify their achievements against agreed criteria.
		Pupils are sometimes asked to discuss each other's work, but this tends to be generalised and the language of feedback is unlikely to be explicit.	Pupils are encouraged to offer feedback to each other in a focused way.	Pupils recognise fully the value of oral feedback and know it is related to their learning. They listen carefully and respond appropriately.	*Pupils have developed a range of strategies to enable them to learn and improve independently.*
		Pupils expect feedback to be at the level of supportive encouragement for participation or urging greater participation.	Pupils expect feedback to be related to their learning so listen to what is said. Pupils do not expect automatic praise but see participation as the norm.	There are beginning to be some clear routines for types of oral feedback.	Pupils recognise that oral feedback is focused on their learning and is as important as written feedback.
			Pupils begin to expect oral feedback and know that they receive specific feedback at certain times, individually or in a small group setting.		Pupils understand well-established routines for group and guided work which involve feedback.

Oral feedback	Pupils	Oral feedback is not specifically expected and is not seen as part of any routine. It occurs almost in passing. It is seen as secondary to written feedback and is not recorded anywhere. *Oral feedback is delivered to the class as a whole and offers little value to individuals.* Pupils will offer comments to each other on their work, but lack clear focus and comments will be general and generally unchallenging.	Oral feedback is beginning to have a distinct value. Pupils are more willing to offer challenging but useful feedback to others.	*Pupils recognise that feedback to others is valuable. They are beginning to develop their questioning skills.* Pupils will readily engage in focused oral feedback to each other and are beginning to develop a vocabulary to do this supported and modelled by the teacher.	Pupils know that feedback to others is valuable and listen carefully. They ask higher order follow-up questions to engage in dialogue. Pupils give regular detailed oral feedback to peers and teachers related to the learning objectives.
Written feedback	Pupils	In some lessons pupils are aware of what they are going to learn in the lesson, but may be unclear of what is expected of them, prior to beginning the task. Written feedback is not easily related to the learning objectives. Pupils rarely act upon feedback.	Pupils are beginning to have a clear idea of what is expected of them through sharing of objectives. Written feedback is understood by pupils to be related to the learning objectives of the task and lesson *(teacher led)*. Feedback is sometimes acted upon. *Pupils begin to think about how this relates to improvement.*	Pupils are beginning to be actively involved in exploring and developing criteria in relation to the learning objective. *Pupils begin to independently connect their feedback to the learning objectives.* Pupils know that action is expected in relation to feedback. Pupils use written feedback to improve their previous performance.	*Pupils expect to be actively involved in exploring and developing criteria in relation to the learning objective. They record the learning objective as part of their work and are confident to review progress in written form against the learning objective.* *Pupils independently connect their feedback to the learning objectives.* Pupils use written feedback to help them reflect on the strengths and weaknesses of their work. They are able to use feedback to set their own targets for improvement.

Key Area		Focusing	Developing	Establishing	Enhancing
Peer and self assessment	Pupils	In some lessons pupils are beginning to gain an understanding of what they are to learn and what they are expected to do to improve their work. There is limited practice of sharing learning objectives and assessment criteria.	Pupils are in the process of developing an understanding of what they are to learn and how they can improve their work using given criteria. Pupils are beginning to assess the work of their peers using the assessment criteria.	Pupils understand what they are doing, how well they have done and how they can improve to attain higher standards. Pupils are able to improve their own and the performance of their peers through an understanding of the learning objectives and assessment criteria.	Pupils are able to independently identify for themselves the skills, knowledge and understanding to move forward. Pupils have an understanding of how they can learn most effectively and are efficient in using assessment criteria.
Curricular target-setting	Pupils	In a few lessons pupils are provided with curricular targets focused on areas of specific underachievement, but the pupils may not use them.	In those departments which have begun to use curricular targets pupils are clearer about their areas of underperformance and how to address them.	Most pupils are beginning to understand their targets in terms of what they are doing, how well they have done and how they can improve their work.	Pupils understand their targets in terms of what they are doing, how well they have done and how they can improve their work. *They are able to identify their own targets to enhance learning.*
Use of assessment data to track progress from Y6 to Y7	Pupils	*Pupils aware of prior attainment levels.*	*Pupils aware of their end of year target level. Pupils achieve short-term targets.*	*Pupils share responsibility with their teacher for setting individual targets and strategies needed to meet targets. Regular review of targets and progress.*	*All pupils set and review achievable yet challenging targets, increasingly requiring less guidance from staff.*
Use of assessment data to track progress in KS3/KS4	Pupils	*Pupils aware of prior attainment levels.*	*Pupils aware of their end of year target level. Pupils achieve short-term targets.*	*Pupils share responsibility with their teacher for setting individual targets and strategies needed to meet targets. Regular review of targets and progress.*	*All pupils set and review achievable yet challenging targets, increasingly requiring less guidance from staff.*

From Meeting the Needs of Your Most Able Pupils: English, Routledge 2007

National Curriculum Key Stage 3 Assessment Criteria for Levels 7 and 8

En 1 Speaking and Listening

Level 7

Pupils are confident in matching their talk to the demands of different contexts. They use vocabulary precisely and organise their talk to communicate clearly. In discussion, pupils make significant contributions, evaluating others' ideas and varying how and when they participate. They show confident use of standard English in situations that require it.

Level 8

Pupils maintain and develop their talk purposefully in a range of contexts. They structure what they say clearly, using apt vocabulary and appropriate intonation and emphasis. They make a range of contributions which show that they have listened perceptively and are sensitive to the development of discussion. They show confident use of standard English in a range of situations, adapting as necessary.

Exceptional performance

Pupils select and use structures, styles and registers appropriately in a range of contexts, varying their vocabulary and expression confidently for a range of purposes. They initiate and sustain discussion through the sensitive use of a variety of contributions. They take a leading role in discussion and listen with concentration and understanding to varied and complex speech. They show assured and fluent use of standard English in a range of situations and for a variety of purposes.

En 2 Reading

Level 7

Pupils show understanding of the ways in which meaning and information are conveyed in a range of texts. They articulate personal and critical responses to poems, plays and novels, showing awareness of their thematic, structural and linguistic features. They select and synthesise a range of information from a variety of sources.

Level 8

Pupils' response is shown in their appreciation of, and comment on, a range of texts, and they evaluate how authors achieve their effects through the use of linguistic, structural and presentational devices. They select and analyse information and ideas, and comment on how these are conveyed in different texts.

Exceptional performance

Pupils confidently sustain their response to a demanding range of texts, developing their ideas and referring in detail to aspects of language, structure and presentation. They make apt and careful comparison between texts, including consideration of audience, purpose and form. They identify and analyse argument, opinion and alternative interpretations, making cross-references where appropriate.

En 3 Writing

Level 7

Pupils' writing is confident and shows appropriate choices of style in a range of forms. In narrative writing, characters and settings are developed and, in non-fiction, ideas are organised and coherent. Grammatical features and vocabulary are accurately and effectively used. Spelling is correct, including that of complex irregular words. Work is legible and attractively presented. Paragraphing and correct punctuation are used to make the sequence of events or ideas coherent and clear to the reader.

Level 8

Pupils' writing shows the selection of specific features or expressions to convey particular effects and to interest the reader. Narrative writing shows control of characters, events and settings, and shows variety in structure. Non-fiction writing is coherent and gives clear points of view. The use of vocabulary and grammar enables fine distinctions to be made or emphasis achieved. Writing shows a clear grasp of the use of punctuation and paragraphing.

Exceptional performance

Pupils' writing has shape and impact and shows control of a range of styles maintaining the interest of the reader throughout. Narratives use structure as well as vocabulary for a range of imaginative effects, and non-fiction is coherent, reasoned and persuasive. A variety of grammatical constructions and punctuation is used accurately and appropriately and with sensitivity. Paragraphs are well constructed and linked in order to clarify the organisation of the writing as a whole.

Bloom wallcharts

KNOWLEDGE
Recalling information
define
label
state
order
recognise
relate

COMPREHENSION
Understanding information
describe
discuss
explain
suggest
express
identify

APPLICATION
Transferring knowledge & understanding
apply
predict
illustrate
dramatise
interpret

ANALYSIS
Making sense of information
analyse
categorise
compare
contrast
differentiate
examine

SYNTHESIS
Combining ideas & making links
summarise
hypothesise
generalise
design
develop

EVALUATION
Making judgements & reasoning
evaluate
argue
prioritise
assess
judge
criticise

 From *Meeting the Needs of Your Most Able Pupils: English*, Routledge 2007

QUADS grid for research

Questions	Answers	Details		Source

From *Meeting the Needs of Your Most Able Pupils: English*, Routledge 2007

KWL chart

What do I know?	What do I want to know?	What have I learnt?

References

Atwood, M. (2002) *Negotiating with the Dead: A Writer on Writing.* Cambridge: Cambridge University Press.

Black, P. (2004) *The Nature and Value of Formative Assessment for Learning.* London: King's College School of Education.

Bloom, B.S. & Krathwohl, D.R. (1956) *Taxonomy of Educational Objectives: The Classification of Educational Goals.* New York: Longman.

Cheshire LA (2004) *Identifying and Providing for Our Most Able Pupils: Cheshire G & T Guidelines.*

de Bono, E. (1985) *Six Thinking Hats.* London: Little, Brown.

de Bono, E. (1992) *Teach Your Child How To Think.* Harmondsworth: Penguin.

Department for Education and Employment (1997) *Excellence in Schools.* London: DfEE.

Department for Education and Skills (2002) *Gifted and Talented Provision: An Overview.* London: DfES.

Department for Education and Skills (2004) *Key Stage 3 National Strategy Pedagogy and Practice Unit 7: Questioning.* London: DfES.

Department for Education and Skills and QCA (2004) *A Condensed Key Stage 3: Designing a Flexible Curriculum.* London: DfES.

Fisher, R. (1998) *Teaching Thinking.* London: Cassell.

Freeman, J. (2001) *Gifted Children Grown Up.* London: NACE/Fulton.

Gardner, H. (1983) *Frames of Mind.* New York: Basic Books.

Goleman, D. (1995) *Emotional Intelligence.* New York: Bantam.

Haddon, M. (2004) *The Curious Incident of the Dog in the Night-Time.* London: Vintage.

Hopkins, D. (2002) *Improving the Quality of Education for All.* London: David Fulton.

Kagan, S. (2001)*Cooperative Learning.* California: Kagan Books.

King, S. (2001) *On Writing.* New York: Simon & Schuster.

Ofsted (2003) *Handbook for Inspecting Secondary Schools.* London: Ofsted.

Ofsted/Audit Commission (2003) *Inspection of Local Education Authorities. Ofsted/Audit Commission Inspection Guidance*, December 2003 v1a. London: Ofsted.

Slavin, R.E. (1994) *Cooperative Learning.* Boston: Allyn & Bacon.

Stoll, L., Fink, D. and Earl, L. (2004) *It's About Learning (and It's About Time) What's In It For Schools.* London: RoutledgeFalmer.

Topping, K. (1988) *The Peer Tutoring Handbook: Promoting Cooperative Learning.* Cambridge, MA: Brookline Books.

Further information

Websites

www.aimhigher.ac.uk

www.alite.co.uk

www.arvonfoundation.org

http://aspirations.english.cam.ac.uk/converse/home.acds

www.bbc.co.uk BBC Education (Bitesize) and BBC News

www.booktrust.org.uk/writingtogether

www.britishdebate.com/debateacademy

www.browningsociety.org

www.citizenshipfoundation.org.uk

www.dyslexiaaction.org.uk

www.esu.org.uk

www.filmeducation.org

www.hefce.ac.uk/widne/summersch

www.londongt.org.uk

www.nace.co.uk

www.nagcbritain.org.uk

www.nagty.ac.uk

www.nc.uk.net/gt

www.newsday.co.uk

www.nyt.org.uk

www.poetrylive.net

www.poetrysociety.org.uk

www.qca.org.uk then use the search facility to go to KS3: English Optional Tasks for the Most Able

www.rcpsych.ac.uk/info

www.shakespeares-globe.org

www.standards.dfes.gov.uk/giftedandtalented

www.teachernet.gov.uk/gtwise

www.teachingenglish.org.uk/think/read/darts.shtml

www.trollopesociety.org

www.worldclassarena.org.uk